COLD ★ WAR
LONG ISLAND

COLD ★ WAR
LONG ISLAND

CHRISTOPHER VERGA & KARL GROSSMAN

THE
History
PRESS

Published by The History Press
Charleston, SC
www.historypress.com

First published 2021

Manufactured in the United States

ISBN 9781467148573

Library of Congress Control Number: 2021943542

Notice: The information in this book is true and complete to the best of our knowledge. It is offered without guarantee on the part of the authors or The History Press. The authors and The History Press disclaim all liability in connection with the use of this book.

CONTENTS

ACKNOWLEDGEMENTS

No one person can own or monopolize the history they write or interpret. The gatekeeper to our history lies in the collective efforts of a community to keep it alive. Whomever we recognize as heroes or villains are defined as such by the effect they had on a community they represented. The Cold War impacted and shaped Long Island physically, politically and economically. The period examined in this book took the young suburbia to its middle ages, when it was struggling to redefine itself.

This book would have not been possible without the help and support of the many people who tirelessly work to preserve this history through image collections and interviews. John Phelan and William Hughes of VFW Post 5350 of Westhampton were staples on creating the veterans' experience prior to the war and after coming home from the war. To the Cradle of Aviation of Nassau County, thank you for the images of the plane crashes and Lunar Module. Thanks to Ralph Weyant for sharing the cover image of the F-14 and for sharing your experiences working with Grumman. We would like to express our gratitude for the images of the student unrest at Hofstra University, Charles Dryden's work in Mitchel Field and access to other related files by Dr. Geri Solomon and Hofstra University Special Collections. These images and documents were essential in our retelling of an almost forgotten history. We would like to extend special recognition to all the local historians we consulted with at the Bay Shore Historical Society, Nassau County Historical Services, Suffolk County Historical Society and the American Air Power Museum.

INTRODUCTION

Pre–World War II Long Island was a series of patchwork towns connected by dirt or limited paved roads that traversed through sporadic downtown centers. The total population of Nassau County in 1930 was 303,053, and the population of Suffolk County was 161,055. The land mass of both counties was dotted with potato farms, landing strips for hobby aviators and large Gilded Age estates that were constructed for some of America's richest families. Similar to other small-town agricultural communities, both counties had a strong isolationist stance, which made the locals oppose any construction for parkway/ expressway systems. The 1930s Long Island economy was based on resorts for New York City residents fleeing the noise and pollution of urban life, a shellfishing industry that yielded prize Blue Point oysters and a budding aviation industry. Nevertheless, within fifty years, Long Island would have one of the most extensive highway systems in the country, and the local stance of isolationism would be beaten back by the increasing demands of a global community. Contributing to these dramatic changes, Long Island developed a military-based manufacturing sector during World War II, which continued into the Cold War era. Further expanding the changes of the landscape were the first postwar suburbs in America. From the dirt and dust of the once-isolated agricultural communities of the early twentieth century rose an endless stretch of Cape Cod houses with manicured lawns and carports. Innovative industries funded by the deep pockets of the U.S. military employed tens of thousands of residents, allowing them to spring into the middle class and distribute their disposable income to various shopping meccas, including Roosevelt Field Mall. With this money circulating in the Long Island economy, an establishment of a top university system took root. The end product was the development of thousands of innovative minds for the generations to come. While the landscape changed and consumerism rose, a social revolution was in the air. Ideas were challenged and communities were tested on the true postwar principles America vowed to uphold. The good guy World War II theme of the United States saving the world from a monstrous global ideology faced the dilemma that the Western economic or government models were not compatible with every society. Post–World War II, the United States started to be called imperialistic when it began trying to impose its ideals globally through its foreign policy. While reflecting on federal policy, collectively the United States struggled with its own demons of racism. Racial covenants socially engineered demographic makeups of communities. Promises of a more just society for the returning Black World War II veterans were not kept. As Long Island was grappling with racial equality and housing discrimination, overpopulation and pollution reminded residents of the island's limits on development. By 1980, Nassau's population had grown to 1,356,582, and Suffolk's population had grown to 1,284,231. The once-proud local shellfish industry became a relic of a bygone era. The culprit of the dying industry was the overflowing septic tanks from mass housing developments leaking nitrogen into the bay, decimating the entire marine ecosystem. The once-amazing coastal bird the osprey that attracted nature lovers' decades prior started to disappear due to the use of DDT as an insecticide. By the late 1980s, cancer rates were on the rise among local residents. The causes were suspected to include the once pristine and ancient aquifers that had remained uncontaminated for thousands of years becoming contaminated in just fifty years due to commercial pollutants.

As the population shifted to a shared fear of an enemy that could strike at any moment, the optimism that paved the way for this economic growth waned. The wave of Cold War prosperity that built Long Island to have a GDP larger or equivalent to other regions would be only temporary and would shift into a pessimism, which reflected the sentiment of the country's crisis of confidence in the late 1970s. This shift would change the political landscape from many people believing in government action to a mixed ideology of libertarian tendency or the least amount of government being best. Further challenges involved a mass migration of high-end manufacturing jobs that would test the resilience of the aging suburbs and put the real estate industry in direct competition with the sunbelt.

World War II birthed modern Long Island, but the Cold War defined the region through understanding that the impossible is possible with commercially based innovation, but at the same time, there were environmental, social and other effects. While balancing the triumphs and setbacks, the World War II values of destroying racism and tyranny did not always apply at home. But with the multilayered history of achievements and contradictions of the Cold War era, Long Island proved it was a collectively resilient region.

1

LAKE SUCCESS FAILURES AT THE UNITED NATIONS

At the close of World War II, Long Island stood out as a potential model for postwar United States. The region had served the country during World War II, becoming an arsenal for democracy that developed cutting-edge military technology and built up a unified war effort. Out of this war effort came a culture with a desire to become a symbol for world peace and human rights. The war manufacturing–based Sperry Plant lay vacant in the village of Lake Success, a symbol of World War II demobilization and future hopes of peace. After World War II, with over 100 million people killed worldwide, the pursuit of peace was the optimistic hope of many. Also, local officials in the village of Lake Success were eager to get the Sperry building back on the tax rolls and generating new commerce. In April 1946, Mayor P. Schuyler Van Bloem met with a search committee that was seeking out a location for the United Nations (UN). The group was eager to find a headquarters for the UN, and Mayor Van Bloem promised a community that would embrace the ideals of the global organization. Similar to embracing the ideals of an American victory in World War II, the UN was birthed by Franklin Delano Roosevelt's Declaration of United Nations, which pledged that signed-on nations would defend and preserve independence, religious freedom and human rights. These shared guiding ideas led twenty-six countries to sign up on January 2, 1942, in agreement to defeat the Axis powers. By the end of the war, a total of forty-six countries had signed on to the treaty, creating a force to lead global peace efforts. On October 24, 1945, the United Nations' formal charter was created, which named five nations as the Security Council, which would hold the most power in votes and vetoing resolutions. One of the five members of the council was the United States. Many locals within the village of Lake Success welcomed the UN as a way to extend postwar patriotic duty.

Before putting the new location to a vote, Rowland Simes, the president of the Lake Success Civic Association, stated, "We have accepted assurance given by the United Nations representatives that they will cooperate in all village matters affecting public safety and contribute a reasonable share of the village taxes."[1] The results of the final vote to rezone the property for the temporary home of the UN was ten to one in favor. On August 29, 1946, the UN building was opened, and in it, the organization held its first session. The first 1,500 delegates from around the world descended on the small village of 700 people. The optimism of some locals in being global citizens and having this symbol of global peace and security in their backyard was short-lived.

The two atomic bombs that were dropped on Japan in August 1945 introduced new fears to the world. One of the first plans of action was to have the United Nations form an Atomic Energy Commission. The top goal of the newly formed commission was to eliminate atomic weapons and inspect atomic energy installations to verify safe use. The countries these restrictions affected the most were the United States because it had developed atomic weapons and the Soviet Union because it was secretly developing its own nuclear arsenal. United States United Nations representative and negotiator Bernard Baruch came up with a compromise. Under the plan, the United States would destroy its entire nuclear arsenal and cease development of future atomic weapons, but in return, the commission would prohibit the production of atomic bombs, seize any global facilities that developed these illegal bombs, impose harsh sanctions against any nations that attempted to develop atomic bombs and restrict all veto power of any nation on blocking any sanctions for violators.[2] The initial twelve-country commission approved the compromise, but the Soviet Union stood in strong opposition and kept the issue adjourned from the United Nations' first session from August into late September. In an effort to pressure the Soviet Union to sign on and not abstain from a vote, attempts were made to get the Soviets to engage in a dialogue. When confronted, Soviet representative Andrei Gromyko stated to the committee, "We are provided limited and incomplete information."[3] On April 1, 1948, the Atomic Energy Commission had adjourned indefinitely, a result of the Russian obstruction. As a result of these failures, the United States House Appropriations Committee passed $150 million in extra funds

Interim Headquarters of the United Nations

United Nations interim headquarters in the Village of Lake Success. *Courtesy of the Great Neck Library Local History Collection.*

for the U.S. Atomic Energy Commission to develop atomic weapons and energy programs. This Soviet hesitation toward the United Nations came with fears that it was a delaying tactic for them to develop its own atomic armament. By August 29, 1949, the Soviet Union had successfully tested its first atomic bomb. When the United Nations confronted the secret success of its first atomic bomb, the Soviet Union's foreign minister Andrei Vishinsky claimed it was using nuclear technology for peaceful energy, not weapons. Vishinsky further elaborated that his country was using atomic energy in "marvelous ways, by spreading life, happiness, prosperity and welfare in places where human footsteps has not been seen for thousands of years."[4] The failure of the United Nations to regulate atomic installations and enforce inspections paved the way for the Soviet Union-United States nuclear arms race, which kept the world on the edge for decades to come.

The arms race was not the only failure of Lake Success. While the Soviet Union delayed action against the Atomic Energy Commission, it built an alliance at the United Nations with Ukraine and Yugoslavia to denounce U.S. warmongering. While making these accusations, the Soviets demanded that the elected representatives of the Korean people be invited to the United Nations to discuss their nation's independence. Prior to October 29,

1947, the United States had a military presence in South Korea, and the Soviets had a presence in North Korea. The dividing line between the two occupying forces was the thirty-eighth parallel, which divided the peninsula down the middle. The United Nations proposed a peaceful transition toward independence for the region, which required Soviet and U.S. troops leaving the nation and United Nations representatives supervising elections. At Lake Success, the Soviet Union protested the United Nations' supervised elections, and in Korea, the communists who were supported by the Soviet Union refused to participate. In response, South and North Korea had separate elections, which designated North Korea as communist and South Korea as capitalist. While the borders between the two regions of influence had been settled, North Korea was planning on unifying the peninsula with the help of the newly formed Chinese communist government. In a secret session at the United Nations, delegates decided who to recognize as the respective Chinese leader and who to fill the Chinese seat on the Security Council. The new communist government seemed hostile and overthrew Chiang Kai-shek's government. Adding to the pressure, the United States declared it would only recognize Chiang Kai-shek's government and would oppose any seating of a communist Chinese representative to the Security Council. The Soviet Union and its satellite countries walked out of the United Nations in protest for not supporting the new Chinese government and tried to work around representation on the Security Council. While this drama played out in Lake Success, America's elected officials had growing concerns about a potential majority communist vote in the United Nations Security Council. While these events were playing out, North Korea invaded South Korea on June 25, 1950, and the United Nations almost immediately authorized Security Council Resolution 83, which had member states intervene. In response to the resolution United States sent ground forces to combat North Korea. By early November 1950, China had sent forces in to back up the North Korean troops. On November 7, Lake Success was full of diplomats from around the world. Fears of a possible world war were further fanned by the recent public protests in the Soviet Union and other communist satellite states. Before the delegates made any decisions, they would have to consider two essential factors: the Soviet Union's attitude toward the United Nations expanding a war with North Korea and communist China and how committed China was to the Korean War.[5] In an unexpected turn of events, Yugoslavia, which allied itself with Soviet Union, announced its support of any United Nations decision taken by the General Assembly. Following the Yugoslavian show of support for any United Nations intervention against China, Soviet foreign minister Vishinsky announced to the member nations that the 300,000 Chinese troops that were assisting North Korea were volunteers and not affiliated with the Chinse government; it further claimed the equipment the volunteers were using against the United Nations and U.S. forces were not supplied by China.[6] In another pivot of the issue, Vishinsky tried focusing on other global issues in order to keep the Chinese intervention in Korea off the agenda. Despite the attempts to shift the blame to outside rebels and change the agenda, United States delegate Warren Austin took to the floor and stated, "If those who are challenging the United Nations believe that we will give up our principles because they threaten us with force, let them know that they are tragically mistaken."[7] Following his statement, Austin moved to sanction the communist Chinese and increase military intervention with his moral argument. With the United States moving to get increased military support, thirteen Asian countries, led by India, moved to start a dialogue with China to stop its military operations at the thirty-eighth parallel.[8] By early January, the UN had come up with a four-stage plan for peace, which included a cease-fire, withdrawal of all non-Korean troops, an interim plan for short-term peace and ongoing negotiations between Korea, the Soviet Union, England, China and the United States for long-term peace. This plan would take almost two years and only achieved an armistice.

The failures of the United Nations played out publicly through failed denuclearization, which resulted in an arms race between the Soviet Union and the United States and the end of a war that killed 33,000 U.S. soldiers in combat and an additional 3,000 who were tortured or starved in North Korean prisoner of war camps. On Long Island, 21 soldiers were declared missing in action and still have not had their remains repatriated to this day. Long Island residents who bore witness to these events shifted their opinion on whether the United Nations was a good fit for Lake Success. Optimism regarding world peace shifted toward militarization, and many lost the desire for global citizenry. U.S. patriotism came in the form of defensive attitudes toward any potential communist ideology. In a reflection of this sentiment, Sperry was reopening its defense manufacturing plants, and it wanted its Lake Success office, then occupied by the United Nations, back. In July 1950, the Sperry Company was in negotiations with the United Nations to take its underutilized space and convert it to a weapons production line. Sperry was prepared to spend $500,000 to convert the selected space to manufacture air instruments, gunfire controls and radar equipment. Sharing an active weapons manufacturing space with an organization that is supposed to represent global peace had conflicts. Within the same year, the

Above and opposite: By 1950, the UN had left Lake Success to relocate to Manhattan. Pictured is the construction of the later UN building. *Courtesy of the New York Public Library.*

United Nations announced the construction of a $65 million thirty-nine-story building in Manhattan. The annual rent Sperry was charging by 1950 ballooned to $202,831 a year for 659,000 square feet of the building. Sperry, under the new agreement, would occupy 50,000 square feet and would later move into a total of 100,000 square feet until the United Nations building was completed entirely. Rent would remain at the same annual rate. Sperry maintained that the immediate need for the space was due to the need to "speedup production to fill order requirements of the Korean conflict."[9] The Sperry plant would later apply more pressure by explaining that the United Nations occupied the building that would be used to employ 5,000 people as compared to the 3,500 employed by the United Nations. Within the village of Lake Success, officials and residents were getting annoyed with foreign diplomats raking up countless amounts of traffic tickets and violations. Instead of paying and having the money generated from the fines reinvested in the community, United Nations officials refused to show up to court or pay the fines under diplomatic immunity protections. The disregard for local law enforcement had residents referring to the workers and diplomats as "United Nations law skirters."

On May 18, 1950, the United Nations flags came down, and the remaining 3,500 workers were shipped to the incomplete United Nations building in Manhattan. By the time the United Nations left, 8,266 meetings had been held there, involving sixty nations, with 1,600,000 visitors annually. The village of Lake Success had visitors that included Eleanor Roosevelt, Warren Austin and Jacob Malik. Guests like Eleanor Roosevelt spread the human rights ideas not just globally but locally when she visited communities across Long Island, such as St. Martin Tours of Amityville, a community that was experiencing its own civil rights struggles. With the locals and elected officials pushing to become part of a global citizenry, five years into the emergence of the Cold War, locals soured to the ideals. A symbol of global peace was quickly retransformed into an international weapons factory.

2

BIRTH OF LEVITTOWN, AMERICA

LIVING ON THE EDGE

The Servicemen's Readjustment Act of 1944, otherwise known as the G.I. Bill, had its greatest economic and social effect between 1945 to 1955. This bill provided funding for veterans to attend college or some type of training program, allowed them to buy a home with no money down and extended a weekly wage of twenty dollars for a year until they found employment. In an effort to reflect growing inflation, Congress increased the G.I. Bill's real estate loan guarantee from $4,000 to $8,000 during the close of the December 1945 congressional session. From New York, over 900,000 residents served in the armed forces during World War II. From the number of New Yorkers who served, 43,000 died in combat. This made New York home to the largest World War II veteran population in the United States. At the end of 1945, demobilization was sped up from 250,000 to 500,000 soldiers being shipped home from the European and Asian theaters of war. The large number of servicemen and women in the New York region all being shipped home at the same time gave New York all the economic benefits of the GI Bill. This influx of returning soldiers created a demand in low-cost housing. In addition to the need for low-cost housing the next 70-million-person baby boomer generation was gradually being born. Throughout the Northeast, Long Island was known as the premier location for the new low-cost housing due to its distance from New York City, surplus land from shuttered defense plants and the availability of farmland due to the infestation of golden nematode worms that devastated Long Island's potato crop. Additional factors that made the island an ideal location for developers was the prewar construction of Southern State and Northern State Parkways, which connected Nassau and Suffolk Counties to New York City by car, an additional option to the aging railroad lines. Developers such as Walter Shirley, William Zeckendorf and Levitt and Sons utilized the existing parkways to design suburbs that were equipped with strip malls centered on locals' accessibility to a car.

Alfred Levitt, the developer of Levittown. He applied a model of assembly line home construction by shipping prefabricated sections of homes to the site of his community and having workers assemble them. *Courtesy of the Nassau County Photograph Archive.*

Alfred and William Levitt, of Levitt and Sons builders, purchased 1,200 acres of land from Island Trees Farm and a surrounding estate for an estimated $300 per acre. The old estate land was purchased from the Merllion Corporation, which was originally owned by Alexander Turner Stewart, a developer of Garden City. The Island Trees land was one of the potato farms that became infested with golden nematodes, making it unusable for potato farming. The developers would apply the model of an assembly-line home construction by shipping prefabricated sections of the homes to the site and having workers assemble them. This method set a record of building thirty-six houses a day. The Levitt houses were originally eight hundred square feet on concrete slabs in a cape or ranch style (ranch styles were offered after 1950).

The homes included built-in televisions, washers and dryers, built-in kitchen appliances and an optional car port. The homes came in five selections of colors but were mostly identical to each other. Each home had a small backyard for hosting play dates or BBQs. The largest developments constructed by Levitt and Sons included a Levittown of Nassau and Bucks Counties, Pennsylvania. The Levittown developments were communities that included public pools, parks, schools, churches and new exit ramps onto existing parkways. Roads were constructed on a curve for a dual purpose of enforcing a slower speed limit and maximizing the greatest number of houses that could be built on a block. The design was marketed as a family-friendly community for the average postwar suburban family. Ownership of a suburban home such as a Levitt house became a status symbol of middle-class success. By 1951, 17,447 homes had been constructed in Levittown,

This page and next: By 1951, 17,447 homes had been constructed on this land and the surrounding property, which comprised parts of Levittown, Wantagh, Hicksville and Westbury. These pictures include aerial and road views of the completed development of Island Tree plots. *Courtesy of the Nassau County Photograph Archive.*

and by the mid- to late 1950s, neighboring East Meadow had over 12,000 homes constructed. The surrounding communities of Wantagh, Hicksville and Westbury, in 1960, had tripled in their population sizes from the prior decade. These communities' most marketable features were the established railroad lines running twenty-five miles from Manhattan and ten miles from the Queens-Nassau border. In 1947, many of the standard two-bedroom homes within these communities retailed, on average, for $6,900. Due to the increase of demand, the price was raised by $1,000 to $7,900. This price point was also based on Congress's revisions to the increased loan guarantees in the G.I. Bill. As a result, Nassau County increased in population from 672,765 in 1950 to 1,300,171 in 1960. Neighboring Suffolk County experienced its own building boom and had a population increase from 276,129 in 1950 to 666,784 in 1960. Towns within Suffolk County, such as Babylon, mostly a farming-based area, experienced the fastest and highest rate of growth. The population of Babylon went from 45,556 in 1950 to 142,309 in 1960. Similar to Nassau County, Suffolk County's developments would bring strip malls and indoor malls. This would bring hundreds of retail jobs and a constant stream of tax revenue for the local towns. These new retail businesses and service industries would fill the lost revenue of the smaller-scale defense plants going out of business following the end of World War II. Suffolk County only maintained three large-scale defense plants: Fairchild Aviation, Grumman in East Islip and Calverton and the East Farmingdale part of Republic Aviation. This commercial revenue would comprise 40 percent of all school tax revenue for many local districts. Revenue of commercial taxes, through large-scale retail or defense companies determined the quality of education for the 125 school districts in Nassau and Suffolk Counties.

The promise of a garden-like community isolated from the dangers of city crime or health hazards that came with high density could not protect residents from a potential international threat. Failures at the Lake Success United Nations Security Council led to the Soviet Union detonating its first nuclear bomb in August 1949. Following the successful test, the United States worked diligently to create a bomb that would burn hotter than 50 million degrees Fahrenheit. The answer came with the successful test of the hydrogen bomb on November 1, 1952. The hydrogen bomb could burn at temperatures as high as 150 million degrees Fahrenheit, or heat estimated to be as high as the sun's interior. The Soviet Union, taking notice, struggled to keep up and detonated its first hydrogen bomb on November 22, 1955. In the development of more powerful bombs, the United States built an estimated total of thirty-one thousand nuclear warheads, and the Soviet Union built an estimated forty-five thousand. It is estimated that only one hundred nuclear warheads detonating at the same time could cause a nuclear winter, which would reduce the Earth's temperatures by putting particles into the atmosphere that could block out the sun.[10] The production of these weapons and the growth of the world's fears were further accelerated when the United States adopted the policy of Mutually Assured Destruction (MAD). This policy ensured if United States was bombed, it would release its nuclear arsenal to achieve full annihilation of the combative force.

In the middle of the arms race escalation, Nassau County civil defense director General Cornelius Wickersham advocated for the county to order and construct bomb shelters. Once he achieved the construction of a county shelter, Wickersham formed a committee composed of County Police Commissioner John Beckmann, Hempstead town treasurer Dr. Michael Leftoff and commander of the Baldwin American Legion post Ralph Verni, which attempted to mandate that all larger buildings constructed in the county have a bomb shelter. The first builder to adopt bomb shelters in all its newly constructed buildings was the Milton Steinberg Company. Steinberg,

Above and opposite: With all of the soldiers coming home, demand was high. Due to the increase in demand, the price was raised by $1,000 to $7,990. For veterans buying a Levitt house, no down payment was required, and the G.I. Bill secured an $8,000 mortgage. *Courtesy of Nassau County Photograph Archive.*

who was contracted to build 250 units of housing projects in Queens, pledged that each residential building would have nine-by-nineteen-foot bomb shelter, and all of Steinberg's new buildings in Nassau would have these shelters as standard equipment. By 1951, all schools in Nassau and Suffolk Counties would be retrofitted with bomb shelters. With the increased price tag of building these new bomb shelters, Governor Thomas Dewey pushed for an emergency aid bill. The finished bill had the state pay 25 percent, the locality pay 25 percent and the federal government pay 50 percent for all new/retrofitted public bomb shelters, and 80 percent of all damage costs in case of an attack would be covered by the state.[11]

Having the state and locality fund 50 percent of the costs of all compulsory shelters drew concerns from many that taxes would increase. In 1959, newly elected New York State governor Nelson Rockefeller had to break the news to the public that state and local taxes would go up on average, $150 annually per household to build the shelters throughout

the state. In a letter to the editor, one Rockefeller supporter stated, "The average American spends $220 for cigarettes and liquor per annum, but we cannot afford $150 which might save our own lives, is plain stupid."[12] In an opposing op-ed, high taxes and expansion of state power were the focus. "The rapidly dwindling store of privacy, individuality and private land ownership concentrating just that much control of private citizens

Left: Government home survival guide for an atomic attack. *Courtesy of the National Archives.*

Opposite: Civil Defense promoted home bomb shelters through advertising or do-it-yourself construction brochures. *Courtesy of the National Archives.*

into the hands of government through compulsory shelters."[13] With the new infusion of tax revenue, Rockefeller, expanded the compulsory bomb shelter plan to include the construction of a shelter for New York State officials. This $4 million shelter would hold 640 people and have the emergency state headquarters inside. While announcing the new state shelter, Rockefeller proposed to further expand the mandated bomb shelters not only for large commercial buildings but for every backyard in Long Island. This proposal would share costs with the state for construction overhead, but it never took root in the state senate or assembly.

In the fall of 1961, Dr. Ralph Lapp, a distinguished nuclear scientist, published a study of what would happen to New York City if a 100-megaton bomb was dropped in midtown Manhattan. The study concluded that the "bomb will dig a hole 400 feet deep and a mile and a half wide, and everyone within seven miles will be killed. All wood-frame houses within 16 miles, which would be as far as Garden City, will be smashed, and radioactive fallout would contaminate 10,000 to 20,000 square miles, which will produce second-degree burns on anyone as far as 35 miles or beyond Huntington."[14] Dr. Lapp further detailed that a shelter underground would be the only way

IMPROVING FALLOUT SHELTER

IMPROVISING A BASEMENT SHELTER

Get a sturdy workbench or table and put it in the corner. Fill boxes or dresser drawers with the heaviest material available.

Stack these materials on the top and at the sides of the table or workbench. It is most important to have overhead protection. Put most of the heavy materials there.

If there is no large table or workbench available, or if more shelter space is needed, place furniture or large appliances in the corner of the basement to serve as the "walls" of the shelter.

As a "ceiling", use doors from the house that have been taken off their hinges. On top of the doors, pile as much shielding material as they will support. Stack other shielding material around the "walls" of the shelter. When everyone is inside the shelter space, block the opening with shielding material.

SHELTER IN STORM CELLARS AND ROOT CELLARS

Storm and root cellars (especially those partially or totally underground) usually provide suitable shelter if they have one foot of soil on the area above ground. If you own or have access to one of them, examine it and make whatever improvements are necessary for your home fallout shelter (including stocking with supplies).

All surfaces above ground level should be covered by at least one foot of soil. Material such as sandbags, bricks, rock, etc. to block the entrances should be available close at hand. In the event you must use the shelter, use this material to close up the entrances so that you have one foot of soil, brick, or rock between you and the outside of the shelter.

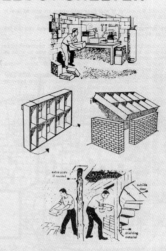

PROTECTION FROM FALLOUT

People can protect themselves against the invisible rays of fallout radiation and have a good chance of surviving it by staying inside a fallout shelter. The mass of the material placed between you and the fallout particles will reduce the radiation, thus protecting you from the likelihood of injury.

The diagram below shows the comparative values of different materials in shielding you from radiation harm. Solid concrete provides the best protection of all the materials shown.

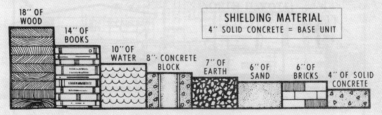

18" OF WOOD
14" OF BOOKS
10" OF WATER
8" CONCRETE BLOCK
7" OF EARTH
6" OF SAND
6" OF BRICKS
4" OF SOLID CONCRETE

SHIELDING MATERIAL
4" SOLID CONCRETE = BASE UNIT

Page Eight

THE FAMILY FALLOUT SHELTER

your one defense against FALLOUT

GET FREE BOOKLET FROM LOCAL CIVIL DEFENSE

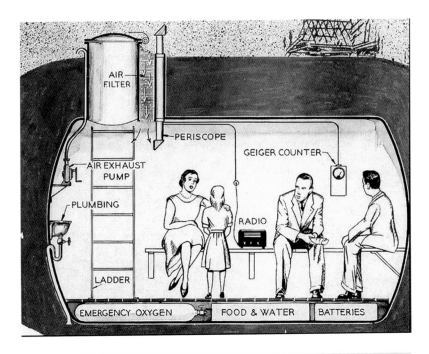

This page: Layouts of a home bomb shelter. *Courtesy of the National Archives.*

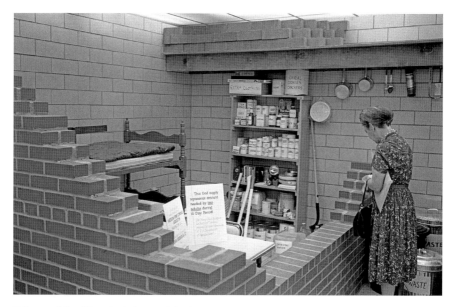

Sales models of bomb shelters, which included supplies of nonperishable food and water. *Courtesy of the National Archives.*

to reduce causalities in such an event. Following this report and Rockefeller's push for a shelter in every backyard, a home shelter construction industry attempted to play on the sense of urgency. The average cost for a shelter was $1,700 with an additional cost of $263 for construction supplies. This industry never picked up, and only an estimated two hundred to three hundred home shelters were built across Long Island.

While local, state and federal officials were trying to find a middle ground on funding community fallout/bomb shelters, public schools started to practice air raid drills. In New York City schools, the 1951 yearly budget added $87,000 to roll out a new annual air raid drill for students and faculty. The same year, with funding from the federal Civil Defense Administration, New York hired the advertising firm Archer Productions to make a kid-friendly instruction film on the school air raid drills. Originally filmed at P.S. 152 in Astoria, Queens, using teachers and students as actors, the film used an animated Bert the Turtle and the easy catch phrase "duck and cover."[15] Bert the Turtle taught a generation of students to duck and cover in routine air raid drills in case of a real nuclear fallout. While New York schools wrote instructional films for students and conducted mandatory drills, other schools around the state and country took on a macabre policy. Schools started issuing dog tags to students that had their names, addresses and religions engraved. The purpose of these tags was to identify the students if they were killed in a nuclear fallout. Long Island schools did not adapt the student dog tag policy, but "duck and cover" was mandated and struggled to take root. The Levittown Educational Association came out against the duck and cover drills, arguing that they could have a physiological impact on the kids. In response, the Nassau County Civil Defense spokesman stated that "only communist policy derides civil defense by ridiculing its necessity in front of the tender impressionable young minds."[16] In response to the public statement provided by the county and in order to prevent a communist fear within the teaching staff, the administration demanded teachers go along with the drills.

On October 16, 1962, a growing conflict between Cuba, a Soviet ally, and the United States took an unsuspected turn into a potential nuclear war. The United States became aware that the Soviets were building nuclear missile sites in Cuba, which is located ninety miles off the coast of Florida. This led to a thirteen-day standoff with open threats from both sides of potentially using their full nuclear arsenal on the other. These thirteen days had all the United States on edge, but the major cities and metropolitan areas were more unsettled, as they were the potential targets. This standoff led to an unexpected push for community demilitarization. Many people started to question whether bomb shelters encouraged war. A *Newsday* editorial stated, "Nuclear warfare resides in the possibility of building a bomb shelter for all its residents to protect them from radioactive fallout and most of all the inability to find a resolution."[17] Other local op-eds stated that Rockefeller's proposals for permanent defense against nuclear warfare displayed an unwillingness to cease nuclear testing and work toward disarmament.[18] Another drastic change was the heighted anxiety of potential communists living in the community and mental health struggles behind closed doors.

Behind the doors of the Cape Cod houses and manicured lawns of Levittown, the U.S. family was going through radical changes. With the nation's soldiers coming home, they brought with them the eyewitness accounts of 85 million or 3 percent of the world's population being killed in either Europe or the Pacific theaters of war. According to the Veterans Administration (VA) 37 percent of the soldiers who were returning home would need psychiatric assistance. While the VA reflected a growth in the need for psychiatric assistance, wartime newlyweds reshaped the norms of marriage. The result of these changes would be that one out of four wartime marriages would end in divorce by 1946.[19] Despite the demand for divorce, New York divorce laws were conservative, and there was no "no fault" as a reason for a legal divorce until the late 1960s. The grounds for a divorce that had to be proven in court were either adultery or cruelty. As the decade and the arms race progressed, a plague of prescription drug addiction took hold in New York and many U.S. suburbs. Households became volatile, with many veterans struggling with war wounds compounded with a fear of nuclear Armageddon. The fear of an impending doomsday and mental health of veterans created an economic boom for Wallace Laboratories, which marketed an antianxiety tranquilizer called Milltown in 1955. This tranquilizer not only reduced anxiety but was highly addictive. Milltown makers quickly hired the marketing firm Ted Bates and Company to promote the drug. Ted Bates and Company was most known for its successful marketing of M&Ms candy. By 1956, many celebrities became open about their use of Milltown; Milton Berle used to make frequent jokes about his use of the drug. In an effort to come up with a more effective and potentially less-addictive drug, benzodiazepines (benzos) were invented. Unfortunately, benzos were stronger and more addictive than Milltown. Both tranquilizers, by 1957, had a total of 35 million prescriptions written a month, which averaged out to one prescription every second throughout the year and a production rate of fifty tons a month.[20] Both drugs became known as "mother's little helpers," with housewives from the 'burbs consuming the largest amounts. While having an average suburban family go through this instability, popular sitcoms, including *Leave It to Beaver, Father Knows Best, Ozzie and Harriet* and *The Donna Reed Show*, portrayed what the manufactured normal family was supposed to be. Father was the head of the household, with decisive leadership over the family and a submissive wife who cooked, cleaned and tended to the needs of her husband. In this manufactured family, the kids were all obedient and conformed to whatever was considered normal within the average suburban community. Many who lived in developments such as Levittown went through mental health struggles and failed to see it represented in popular media, which made many families feel isolated within their own communities. Women who had trouble adapting to the manufactured 1950s family through homemaking were labeled neurotic or sometimes schizophrenic by many mental healthcare professionals.[21]

Mental health struggles were not the only things plaguing the new postwar Long Island. The fundamental principles of "all men are created equal" were pushed aside by banks and developers. Levitt advertised in many media publications throughout the tristate area that home applications would be processed based on veteran's preference. But what was left out of these advertisements and interviews was he only meant White veterans. Levitt and

Sons barred Black families from renting its homes and racially steered Black families out of buying its homes. Allies of Levitt and Sons included local banks, which refused to provide or process VA mortgages to Black home buyers seeking houses in Levitt developments. For renting with the option to buy, Levittown's leases had clause twenty-six, which stated, "The tenant agrees not to permit the premises to be used or occupied by any person other than members of the Caucasian race, but the employment and maintenance of other than Caucasian domestic servants shall be permitted." This clause was enforced through evictions and steep fines to the landlords if the homes were privately owned. This newly designed postwar suburb and its policies had the relic of institutionalized segregation bestowed by local Ku Klux Klans decades prior. Local Klan members of the 1920s were owners of home maintenance companies, banks, residential insurance companies and local real estate firms. Many civil rights groups claimed the former Klan members did not disappear; rather, they merely transitioned into the early 1950s by trading in their white garments for suits and becoming developers. This 1950s racial ideology did not teach that there was an inferior race, but it argued economic advantages through real estate values. In a 1958–60 survey conducted among three Levittown developments (Levittown, New York; Levittown, Pennsylvania; and Levittown, New Jersey) as to why residents relocated to Levittown; only 4 percent cited racial change of a prior neighborhood as the most important reason, but 20 percent checked off racial change as one of the reasons.[22] The redlining of banks, racial clauses and racial steering were argued as ways of preserving increasing home values. Feeding into these practices and other ingrained biases, many middle-class White homeowners either remained silent on these issues or aggressively encouraged them. These race-based real estate policies were ruled illegal in 1948 with the U.S. Supreme Court case *Shelley v. Kraemer*. The *Shelly v. Kramer* case ruled that racial restrictive covenants were a violation of the Fourteenth Amendment's equal protection clause. This ruling further put a ban on any funds provided by the Federal Housing Administration that would have gone to housing or loans that upheld any restrictive clauses. This ruling should have deterred race-based practices, as the Federal Housing Administration funded the bulk of all mortgages in Levittown. The continuation of racial restrictions despite the *Shelly v. Kraemer* ruling was the foundation of the second civil rights movement.

Nationally, an estimated 1.2 million Black people served during World War II, with the guiding idea that they were ending tyranny. However, upon returning home, Black people all over country and on Long Island found the same conditions they had endured prior to World War II. Fighting tyranny abroad did not extend to ending racial oppression at home. Returning Black troops demanded equality and wanted the ideal American dream that returning White soldiers were given. Mortgage lending, quality schools, fair/equal employment and anything that would provide a pathway to the middle class was every Black veteran's guiding ideals for the second civil rights movement. Donald Archer and his mother, Myrtle Archer, from Jamaica, Queens, tried buying a house in Levittown in early 1953. Donald, a veteran, would have been approved for any VA loan and had the qualified income. When they went into the sales office, however, they were told that "we are not selling to Negroes at this time." In an interview with *Newsday* relating to Donald Archer's attempt to buy a Levitt house, a spokesperson for Levittown stated, "Our policy as to whom we sell or do not sell is the same as that of any other builder in the entire Metropolitan area." Many local 1950s civil rights leaders were rejected from buying a home in Levittown. Eugene Burnett and Irwin Quintyne, both honorably discharged, were told by Levittown sales managers that "we were not selling to Negroes at that time." The resulting anger mobilized Quintyne and Burnett. Quintyne became the leader of the Congress of Racial Equality (CORE), and Burnett became part of the local National Association for the Advancement of Colored People's (NAACP) leadership.

These racial boundaries were finally broken when another Black veteran, William Cotter, had a White friend sign the lease for him and his family to get into Levittown. In 1953, Cotter was evicted based on his violation of clause 26. Cotter would fight his eviction, and his case would eventually be brought to the New York State Supreme Court, which, in 1959, ruled that he was permitted to rent and later buy a home in the development. With state courts ruling in favor of William Cotter, CORE became inspired to be a force against housing discrimination. Members of CORE would go to local real estate firms and test their housing equity by sending Black people into the firm and asking for the availability of apartments in white communities. Many locals, in response, underplayed the civil rights leaders' efforts as communist agitation. CORE members were labeled as communists or crackpots. One member, John Moscow of Oceanside, was awarded the National Merit Scholarship. Locals complained to Oceanside High School that a communist should not get any of the scholarship money, and his school peers would throw food at him and call him a "dirty Jew communist bastard."[23] Other civil rights organizations, such as the Levittown-Wantagh Committee for Brotherhood, were publicly denounced as communist organizations and were blocked from speaking in any community forums within Levittown. This local civil rights group of seventy to two hundred people drew the attention of Operation Suburbia, which had local volunteers host inner-city minority kids for a summer to enjoy the amenities of Nassau County.[24] In an effort to intimidate the Levittown-Wantagh Committee for Brotherhood, CORE and other civil rights groups, local youths who were Barry Goldwater supporters and anticommunists became part of an anti-integration group called the Society for the Prevention of Negroes Getting Everything (SPONGE). The group formed chapters in the Levittown, Hicksville and East Meadow communities. SPONGE originated in New York City's White working-class communities, and it protested new families of color moving in through picketing, vandalism or bullying.[25] On Long Island, SPONGE counterprotested all CORE demonstrations. During a CORE protest that led a five-hundred-person rally against housing discrimination at Vigilant Associates in Hicksville, SPONGE counterprotested by carrying Confederate flags and holding signs of support for Barry Goldwater, with racial slurs comparing CORE to communist agitators. The event was later broken up by police due to bomb threats that were believed to come from other racist groups. These other racist groups included the Taxpayers and Parents Association. This group would generate a misinformation campaign that argued against school and community integration. The arguments generated through the Taxpayers and Parents Association held that integrated schools led to lower standards and reduced property values. This misinformation further escalated racial tensions, and many conservative locals constructed a more stigmatized communist label for civil rights workers. The communist title was used against these groups because it was evolving as a weaponized term due to the shared anxiety of the Soviet enemy.

While many communities across Long Island were fighting integration, one developer, Thomas Romano, was trying to embrace the guiding idea that "all men are created equal." Purchasing 147 acres of land in North Amityville, Romano built over one thousand homes. The marketing of these homes was advertised as resisting the "undemocratic restrictions of race, color or creed." This development became known as Ronek Park. For many Black soldiers who were turned away from developments such as Levittown, this community became not only a vestige for civil rights principles but a path to the American middle-class family.

While the Long Island suburbia reshaped the traditional family, masked mental health through tranquilizers and became a new battleground for civil rights struggles, Cold War threats of nuclear annihilation remained dominant in most Americans' minds. These fears would shift politics and the local economy for decades to come. The urgency created through fears of nuclear annihilation would make conservative nuclear war hawk views of expanding a nuclear arsenal unpopular. In the 1964 election, while running against Lyndon Johnson, Barry Goldwater famously stated that generals should have nuclear authority in combat and that nuclear weapons should be considered in the growing conflict in Vietnam. In response, Johnson would win Suffolk and Nassau Counties with over 50 percent of the vote. Goldwater's nuclear war hawk message caused him to lose every county in New York State, and he only won the states of Arizona, Mississippi, Louisiana, Alabama, Georgia and South Carolina. The remaining forty-four states went to Johnson. But with public opinion opposed to the use or buildup of nuclear weapons, polls did not reflect an antiwar or anti–global intervention policy. In a 1963 GALLUP poll, 84 percent of Americans expected and felt it was of "great importance" that the United States increase its power throughout the world. These polls were aligned with defense spending, which kept contracts flowing to Long Island's largest defense plants.

3
MILITARY INDUSTRIAL COMPLEX
OF LONG ISLAND

During World War II, Long Island became the arsenal for democracy. Fighter planes such as the Hellcat, Avenger and the P-47 Thunderbolt contributed to an Allied victory and pushed the historic agricultural communities of Long Island into a bygone era. Farmingdale's Republic Aviation held the record for the most-manufactured fighter plane, the P-47 Thunderbolt. In total, 15,579 P-47s were built, with a record amount of 6,500 being shipped out for delivery in eighteen months. The innovation Republic introduced was the focus on the man-hours used to create each plane. When production first began for the Thunderbolt, the average man-hours to construct one plane was 22,927, but by 1944, the company set a goal (and achieved the goal) to get this time cut to 7,729.[26] This reduction of man-hours created a cheaper overhead, which made the price of the plane drop from $83,000 to $68,000 per plane. This drop in production costs allowed the company to bid on additional military contracts. Grumman, following this model, became the other manufacturing giant to dominate the military aircraft industry on Long Island. But despite the size of these plants, dozens of other plants competed for the same contacts. On May 8, 1945, Germany surrendered, and three months later, on August 14, Japan also surrendered. Following the announcement of a Japanese surrender, all war-based manufacturing plants put their workers on a V-J holiday. Spokespeople from these collective plants, including Ranger Aircraft, Sperry Gyroscope Company, Grumman, Columbian, Liberty Aircraft and Republic Aircraft, stated, "There will be no layoffs, and everyone will return to work; enjoy the holiday at home with your community and family." But across the country, these war manufacturing holidays were designed for management to assess the size, profitability and effectiveness of their workforce.

A few days after the announcement of the holiday and the promises of no layoffs, Republic notified all its workers not to return to work until they were notified by management. Despite the layoffs pride of constructing the planes that won the war redefined the local culture and was reflected throughout the local communities. In a few short years, the high schools that surrounded the plants renamed sports teams to reflect the planes, such as the Wildcats, Thunderbolts and Avengers. The identity of growing communities, such as Bethpage, Farmingdale, Hicksville, Bellmore, Merrick, Wantagh, Hempstead, and other villages and towns, became dependent on the tax revenue and disposable income generated from these plants' military contracts. This buildup of a military manufacturing-based economy would have localities build and expand public work projects and public-school vocational programs and harness a budding retail-based economy through the construction of small plazas and large-scale malls. In addition to expanding the community's economic growth, women and Black residents were able to start making inroads to the middle class due to the demand for manufacturing employees and state/federal executive orders that cracked down on employment discrimination. Further cementing the efforts of federal executive orders, Governor Thomas Dewey signed the Ives-Quinn Anti-Discrimination Bill on March 12, 1945. This bill made employment discrimination illegal and established the New York State Commission Against Discrimination to investigate complaints. But all of these economic gains, which Long Island was dependent on, were then in danger of being dismantled due to the area's inability to transition to a peacetime economy. By the end of August, over 5 million defense plant workers across the country had been laid off, and the country faced a labor glut with falling wages. With the economic fallout on Long Island and in other manufacturing-based communities, President Harry Truman expressed optimism in his speeches. Truman explained that these economic setbacks were due to transitioning from a war-based economy to a peacetime economy. Suffolk and Nassau Counties struggled to get the smaller defense plant properties that became abandoned back on their tax rolls. The overall answer was to rezone the properties for residential or retail use. In an attempt to shift from a manufacturing-based economy to a service-based economy, permits and plans for large-scale malls were approved with no resistance from town planning and zoning boards. But with rising tensions between the United States and the Soviet Union, there was an uptick in demand for new designed fighter planes and other military components. The large- and medium-scale plants that survived the end of the war were Liberty, Fairchild, Republic, Sperry and Grumman Aircraft Manufacturing. These aircraft companies would become stronger following the closures of competing companies, and they become even more profitable.

REPUBLIC AVIATION

Post–World War II Republic attempted to get into the civilian market for aviation. In 1946, Republic received a contract from American Airlines to deliver twenty of its civilian XF-12 Rainbow Airliners. This plane was originally being developed for the United States Army for surveillance, but with the close of the war, it was seen as an opportunity for the company to break into a peacetime economy. On February 24, 1947, American Airlines canceled its contract with Republic. A fraction of the size it was prior to the close of the war, Republic laid off 837 more workers. Later in the year, Republic laid off an additional 1,000 workers, and at a press conference, company president Mundy Peale told reporters, "The nation's entire aircraft industry is in for an early death unless current trends are reversed."[27] But Republic was about to discover that this slump was temporary and that tensions in Korea were turning into a full-scale war. With these tensions and preexisting distrust of the Soviets' militarization, civilian focus was shifted back to military contracts.

Prior to the close of World War II, military aviation in Germany was experimenting with jet-powered aircraft, which redesigned fighter plane motors to become airbreathing engines. This airbreathing engine would replace a standard propeller with an axial compressor that utilized pressurized gases. Nazi engineers who experimented with axial compressors in engines were sought out by U.S. aviation manufacturers. With the onset of tensions with the Soviet Union, the United States cemented its lead in aviation by using the new airbreathing methods in engines. To monopolize the trade secrets of this method, the United States implemented Operation Paper Clip. Nazi war criminals Anselm Franz, who experimented with the turboshaft, and Hans von Ohain, who constructed the first turbojet, were put to work at the American Institute of Aeronautics and Astronautics.

In seeking nefarious aviation engineers, President Eisenhower created the Defense Advanced Research Projects Agency (DARPA) in the late 1950s. DARPA injected funding for innovative ideals or advanced research that could benefit the military. With a rebound of orders due to hysteria over the growing tensions with the Soviet Union and with the Korean War on the horizon, military manufacturing companies that were on life support following the end of World War II started to report record-setting profits.

Long Island Republic Aviation reemployed many of its workers to start constructing the F-84 Thunder Jet, the first of a series of jet fighters. This fighter plane was the first to have in-flight refueling abilities and an ability to carry a nuclear bomb. The top speed for the F-84 was an impressive 620 miles per hour, and it had six M2 Browning machine guns in its nose and on its wings. The newly formed United States Air Force put an order in for 7,500 F-84s in 1947 at a cost of $250,000 to $750,000 each. With the success of the F-84, a series of similar models with the same main components of the Thunder Jet's engine were developed. In mid-1950, Republic developed the F-84F Thunderstreak and the RF-84F Thunderflash. In total, more than 3,000 F/RF-84F jets were produced.

The F-84 was one of the first mass-produced fighter planes after Republic's reorganization after World War II. *Courtesy of the U.S. Air Force Museum.*

With the new age of fighter jets, it was hard to keep up with demand and evolving technology. On October 14, 1947, Chuck Yeager broke the sound barrier in his Bell-X-1 Jet. The speed required to break the sound barrier is over seven hundred miles per hour. In an effort to put the performance of the F-84 to shame, Republic set out to develop a supersonic jet in 1951. Republic's engineering team developed its first supersonic jet, the F-105 Thunderchief, in 1955. The F-105 had a Pratt & Whitney J75-P-19W engine that had a twenty-four-thousand-pound thrust. Its top speed was an unimaginable eight hundred miles per hour, and it had a 600-mile-per-hour cruising speed. Later, Thunderchief Jets developed a top speed of one thousand miles per hour. The fighter jet's armament included a M61 20-millimeter cannon and the ability to carry fifteen thousand pounds of ordnance. In total, 830 of the Thunderchiefs were built at a price of $2 million each.

With Republic's successful innovation of the Thunder and supersonic jet series, its demand expanded into global markets. North Atlantic Treaty Organization (NATO) member countries placed multimillion-dollar orders. By 1955, Republic had built more than one-third of all combat aircraft used by the U.S. Air Force, and its fighters had grown in demand, with sixteen additional air forces around the world as new customers.[28] To meet demand, the production of the Farmingdale plant yielded an average of three and a half jets a day.

In 1954, Republic had net sales of $323,456,601 a year, but by 1955, it had netted $547,387,242. This increase beat all expectations, as the last American conflict, the Korean War, had ended in 1953. Making this push to an unimaginable expectation was Republic's army of 1,900 engineers, 585 suppliers and 285 subcontractors around Long Island who maintained the speed of production. The growing production expanded the Republic Farmingdale plant to 2,900,000 square feet within a 587-acre facility.[29] This new growth at Republic was spurred not only by the constant flow of government contracts but by the 12,000 highly skilled employees who delivered the highest quality of workmanship to fill orders on time. Understanding the collective wealth of the workers, the manufacturing floor's labor was unionized under the powerful American Federation of Labor (AFL). The AFL understood that the workers were the backbone of the company and used this as leverage in collective bargaining. Despite the union's strength and the efficiency of the workers' output, Republic's management stayed focused on maximizing profits and keeping the possibility of a merger open between itself and the competing Fairchild Aviation. These management goals kept the union in a constant power struggle with Republic.

The F-105 Thunder Chief was Republic Aviation's first jet to reach Mach-two speeds. *Courtesy of the U.S. Air Force Museum.*

The first of a series of power struggles came with a stalled wage increase. The demands to reinstate the promised wage increase erupted between Republic's union and the company's management in late May 1952. In addition, the company's management fired and suspended eighty of the most vocal and active union members, claiming that they were "rebel employees." The management's purge came on the heels of the new appointment of Martin Buckley as the new union head. The following day, Buckley called an emergency meeting with the delegates at the Elks Club in Hempstead. While in talks with the management and delegates, eight thousand of the company's twelve thousand workers went on a "wildcat strike." Once the workers went on strike, a federal mediator was appointed to get the employees back to work. George McGahan, the federal mediator, blamed the unauthorized strike on Buckley and said he was willing to conference but that it "would be purely explorative as to what caused the strike and there will be no established agenda."[30] Following the two-day strike, the union and management came up with a settlement that restored the employment of dismissed workers but left the wage dispute for a later time. But as successful bidding of military contacts and new innovations in the sonic jets progressed, Republic's labor force expanded with stalled wage growth. Other company practices that drew the attentions of the labor unions included the laying off of workers based on the completion of government contracts and rehiring workers on the next awarded contract. By early 1954, the floor labor force had grown to fifteen thousand workers, and a total of twenty-nine thousand people were employed by all four Republic plants. The more organized union, International Association of Machinists, Republic lodge, was demanding wages and benefits to reflect the increasingly higher cost of living. Before the old contract between Republic and the union expired in February 1954, the union laid out its demands publicly. These demands included a $0.25-per-hour wage increase, four additional paid holidays and increased insurance benefits.[31] After twenty-nine hours of intense negotiations, a contract was proposed and then ratified the following day. The new contract gave a wage boost of $0.05 to $0.10 per hour, a fifteen-year or sixty-five-years-of-age pension and a guarantee against layoffs.[32] The layoff clause was the toughest part of the agreement for Republic to honor.

In the mid-1950s, Republic was putting all its resources toward diversifying its products. Republic was given the rights to market and produce the French helicopter Alouette. In addition to creating a helicopter production line, the company innovated a new gyroscope to compete with Sperry. This attempt in diversification put the company in the red from the start. By 1956, the attempts to build additional divisions had led to a backlog of $500 million worth of the company's flagship fighter jets. With the backlog, tensions between the management and the union were on the rise. The management at Republic was using loopholes to lay off workers or threaten to lay off workers if they did not take a lower-grade position with a lower wage. Many of the employees felt insecure economically, and the company shifted the blame to the union's demands. Despite the threats of demotions, layoffs and shifting blame, by 1956, 29,000 employees were represented through multiple unions that ranged in size. The largest in membership was the International Association Machinists, which had over 10,000 members, and the smallest was the Brotherhood of Electrical Workers, which had 150 active members. These unions were not fragmented but unified on guiding ideals, and they had the policy that if one union went on strike, they all went out on strike. In addition to this, the local unions that represented Republic expanded to represent the workers in subcontractor companies, such as Republic's neighbor Fairchild aircraft.

In February 1956, the labor contract was near its expiration, and the unions wanted layoff protection, to have workers recalled with no loopholes and a $.038-an-hour raise in wages. After closed-door meetings with the company, the union dropped the $.038 raise to $0.19, and the management's counteroffer was a $0.05-an-hour raises with no clear response to the other demands. The union rejected the counteroffer, and the management refused any further negotiation. While the union was hitting this roadblock at Republic, a similar stalled dialogue was happening at Fairchild. In response, all the unions that were representing Republic workers and most of the unions representing Fairchild workers declared a strike. Production screeched to a halt. Republic remained on strike for more than 105 days; Fairchild's striking workers returned in just over a month. Fairchild management agreed to hire back the laid-off workers from a month prior and agreed to more talks with the union to establish a middle ground. On the eighty-ninth day of Republic's strike, the Senate and House of Representatives attempted to weigh in with their influence. Congressman Stuyvesant Wainwright of New York's first congressional district stated, "The Senate subcommittee has a perfect right to investigate any phase of work on a defense contract due to national defense. But the job action of the union was not jeopardizing the pentagon and would provide federal intervention at this time."[33] This lack of federal intervention and the further investigation of Republic in the House of Representatives and an additional investigation picking up on war profiteering put the company at a disadvantage. By June 2, the strike was near an end. The largest union, the International Association of Machinists, said it would not agree to any terms of the strike until the company came to terms with the smaller 150-man electric workers' union, closed the loopholes in the layoff protections and recalled all laid-off workers. The company countered, saying all employees who had been laid off would have a two-day notice and two days' worth of pay. All other employees would get $0.16-an-hour raise over the next two years.[34] As the strikers went back to work, the weaknesses of Republic's management and failed attempts to diversify became public, and the company was prime for a corporate takeover or merger. In early 1958, Republic hit a slump in contracts, which came in the form of 3,000 layoffs. The largest cause of the slump was the air force canceling a $100 million contract for the XF-103 jet that was in middle of development. The XF-103 would have potentially reached a speed of Mach three and had a flight ceiling of eighty thousand feet (if it had been developed).

While enduring these cuts, a smaller subcontractor, Liberty Aircraft, would lay off 100 workers. Liberty vice-president John Taggart, in a company conference, stated, "Republic's layoffs were sort of a chain reaction. When large aircraft firms, which give about 95 percent of our work, are affected, it hits us sooner or later."[35] Sperry and Grumman had layoffs as well, but

The Republic XF-103 became a canceled contract, which sent Republic into an economic tailspin. *Courtesy of the U.S. Air Force Museum.*

one company was expanding and adding employees. Fairchild secured contracts for air force missiles and components such as pressure regulators. Fairchild's Guided Missiles Division of Wyandanch lost only 200 jobs, but it expanded its Engine Division in Deer Park from 1,600 workers to 2,400, and the Stratos Pressure Regulator Division of Bay Shore grew from 1,000 workers to 1,280. Despite the federal aviation contract cuts, Fairchild was economically solvent in comparison to all of its larger competitors.

On January 5, 1959, the United States government awarded a missile contract to Grumman, Republic and Fairchild in an effort to collaborate on designing a long-range missile that could potentially reach other planets. This was the birth of the space race, and the federal government was determined to surpass the Soviets in the race to the moon. This new endeavor comprised eleven specific contracts related to the new missile project and an additional $5 billion in developing a drone surveillance program.[36] These new contracts made up 35 percent of Republic's yearly sales and became the rebound the company needed to recover from the losses of the stalled helicopter production line. Working with Fairchild had unintended consequences. While teaming up, the structural weaknesses in the company were revealed to the one-time rival, and the prospects for a merger became more lucrative. Prior to Fairchild's move on a merger, Republic was likely

This page: The Fairchild Aircraft Stratos Pressure Regulator Division of Bay Shore. *Courtesy of the Library of Congress, Image Collection.*

to buy out Fairchild. Six years prior, in 1954, Republic bought the Fairchild Engine and Airplane Division for close to $4 million, which was the one of the largest business deals in Long Island's aviation history.[37]

In the early 1960s, corporate competitive strength shifted. Toward the close of the 1950s, Fairchild Aircraft started buying up shares of Republic. By August 1964, Fairchild bought out Hiller Aircraft in an effort to shift production at a cheaper cost. With these savings and increased stock value, Fairchild had enough money to make its next power play. This came on September 30, 1965, when Republic's remaining 1,459,457 stocks were bought for $14.50 a share by Fairchild. The grand total of the merger was $44,400,000. All remaining property and assets were transferred to the Fairchild Corporation. And within a week of the merger, Republic was able to secure a $30 million subcontractor contract for McDonnell Aircraft Corporation. This contract would deliverer fuselages for the F/ RF-4 Phantom Fighter Jet. In addition to accepting subcontracts, Fairchild downsized Republic's facilities. Republic's flagship planes the F-105, which had utilized an 18,000-man workforce for the past nine years, would cease all production. As a result, 14,000 workers were laid off. Republic's airport and its hangers, which took up 265 acres, employed 3,700 people and contributed to $750,000 a week in payroll for the company, became the next potential cut for Fairchild.[38] In an effort to keep the property on the tax rolls and add an additional airport to the county, the regional planning board of Suffolk County purchased the property for the full market value of $8 million. Republic designed its last successful Thunder Fighter Jet in 1972. The Fairchild A-10 Thunderbolt II, later referred to as the Warthog, would have a top speed of 430 miles per hour and could fly as high as forty-five thousand feet. Designed to be more mobile in lower altitudes, the A-10 cost the United States $18 million per plane The prototypes were built in Farmingdale Republic, which energized the innovation of the plant, but despite the successful prototypes, the remaining 714 planes were built in the Fairchild plant in Maryland. The Fairchild A-10 Thunderbolt II is still used by the military as of 2021.

GRUMMAN

Similar to Republic, Grumman was in an economic death spiral, which included falling sales and cancellations of military contracts. At its peak during the war, Grumman employed twenty-five thousand workers. At the end of the war, Grumman scaled back its workers to just over five thousand. Toward the end of the war, Grumman partnered with subcontractor Columbia Aircraft Corporation to design and build an amphibious plane. The Columbia XJL was on track to retire the military's Grumman J2F Duck, but the war ended, and the contract was canceled. In an attempt to keep the company profitable and not close down all production, the Grumman G-73 Mallard was built with a similar design, but it had more of a modern turboprop engine. Unfortunately, the civilian market did not catch on, and only fifty-nine were produced. But with the rising tensions of the Cold War, Grumman modified the Mallard to fill a military contract for air and sea planes. This plane became known as the HU-16 Albatross.

With international tensions on the rise and an almost certain war in Korea, the stalled production of Grumman planes such as the F7F Tigercat resumed. The Tigercat, originally developed in late 1944, was stalled due to a cancellation of military contracts, but with growing tensions, 350 were needed. This plane was built to be a bomber that was able to fly at longer ranges, and it was adopted by the military for surveillance. As demand for military aircraft picked up, Grumman started developing its new jet fighter plane to cut into Republic's turbo jet market share. As Republic developed

The Columbia XJL would be modified to become the postwar Grumman G-73 Mallard. *Courtesy of the Cradle of Aviation Museum of Nassau County, Image Collection.*

its F-84 Thunder Jet, the F9F Panther would be an attempt to get back into the military market in late 1947. In total, 1,382 Panthers were produced before Grumman redeveloped the plane into the F-9 Cougar. The Cougar had a cursing speed of 647 miles per hour, in contrast to the earlier Panther's 579 miles per hour. This plane's best feature was the rumored top speed of 800 miles per hour. But the headlines that held the most interest said that this F-9 would be built in the new navy plant in Calverton.

On November 24, 1950, the navy started surveying an area of ten farms and a section of the old Woolworth Estate that encompassed a scrub oak brush forest within the rural town of Calverton. For little under a year, first congressional district congressman Ernest Greenwood was petitioning the navy to consider building a manufacturing plant in his district. The constant requests for the plant paid off in early 1951, when the navy finalized a plan to purchase 6,000 acres of this surveyed Calverton property. This tract of land became a state-of-the-art weapons plant and an airport later known as the Grumman Peconic River Airport. The expansion of this plant was not popular among local farmers, and by 1953, Greenwood was voted out, and Stuyvesant Wainwright became the new congressman for the district. Once elected, Wainwright started to probe the land sales. Grumman and the navy then had 3,000 acres of the original 6,000-acre goal, but they were largely undeveloped. Adding to the original 6,000-acre goal, the navy purchased 4,400 acres, which displaced many local farmers. Wainwright petitioned the navy to sell the land back to farmers and to consider the Brookhaven Laboratory's surrounding acreage that had remained undeveloped under the ownership of the United States Army. Between the political infighting, resistance from local farmers and the slow construction of the plant buildings, Grumman partially constructed the F-9 Panther and modified model the F-9 Cougar on the new facility grounds. Between both F-9 models, over three thousand were made in the Bethpage or the new Calverton Plants. Later, the navy would reserve 1,000 acres of the plant property to create the Calverton National Cemetery. With the development of these flagship planes and the expansion of government property, the Town of Riverhead was growing concerned over the lost tax revenue on the smaller parcels of land. The land was utilized by Grumman, which was subject to being taxed, but the navy owned the property. In 1955, Riverhead assessed the surrounding acreage and the plant at $743,100, which came out to a tax bill of $60,000 that was owed to Riverhead. Appealing the tax bill, State Appellate Court Judge Howard Hogan ruled in favor of Grumman. Hogan ruled, "Riverhead hasn't the right to tax Grumman for 1954–55 taxes because the aircraft company

This page: A Grumman E-2 Hawkeye at the Calverton Grumman plant. *Courtesy of Christopher Verga.*

doesn't have a true option to buy the government-owned installation and currently rents the federally owned plant."[39] While the town was suffering defeat in court for collecting local taxes, the navy announced it would buy more land in an effort to "prevent fights similar to those which took place at Mitchel Field Air Force Base, where building booms led to residential development of the surrounding airfields, resulting in new hazards due to the new populated residential communities."[40] The total amount of land the navy wanted for a safety buffer would have been 9,600 acres. The proposed buffer would include popular Boy Scout Camp Wauwepex and displace several family farms. With pushback from the community and Congressman Wainwright attempting to block the $8,487,000 spending bill for the navy, the proposed buffer was scaled back.

In July 1959, the navy and Grumman had their first large scale test flight. The YAO-I Mohawk, tested and built by the Calverton plant, had a top speed of three hundred miles per hour but was designed for the primary purpose of surveillance. In total, Grumman filled an order of 380 planes. This plane was the start of a series of Grumman developments that carried the company into a wave of economic success for the next twenty years. The following year, Calverton developed another surveillance plane called Grumman E-2 Hawkeye. The Hawkeye had an airborne warning and control system that was designed to detect radar from submarines and other marine vehicles. Similar to the Mohawk, the Hawkeye had a top speed of three hundred miles per hour, and a total of 313 were made. This plane had such an effective design that it is still in American military service today.

A Grumman F-14 Tomcat firing an AIM-54 Phoenix missile. *Courtesy of National Archives and Records.*

An AIM-54 Phoenix missile in Calverton Grumman Memorial Park. *Courtesy of Christopher Verga.*

The successful development of the Hawkeye was dwarfed by the premier iconic Cold War–era plane, the F-14 Tomcat. The sticker price for the United States Air Force was $19.2 million per plane. For $19 million, the F-14's top speed was Mach two or 1,500 miles per hour, and it could reach an altitude of 50,000 feet and had range of 1,600 miles. But its most impressive feature was its radar system. The F-14, designed in 1970, was equipped with the first microprocessors, which gave the radar the ability to track up to 24 planes at the same time, and it had an additional AWG-9 X-band pulse doppler radar.[41] This feature provided radar guiding on the long-range missiles. The exclusive long-range missile was the Raytheon Corporation's AIM-54 Phoenix. The accuracy of the Phoenix was 77 percent, but its feature that stood out the most was its programable data and ability to be deployed toward multiple targets. While the orders for this plane were coming in, Grumman was starting to face slowing profitability. The United States ordered 334 planes for a total contract price of $6.4 billion, and Iran ordered 80 for a price of $2 billion (the Iran order came before the Islamic Revolution of 1979). In an effort to fill these contacts and not lay twenty-two thousand workers off, Grumman got a commercial line of credit in the amount of $200 million from an Iranian state-owned bank and American banks.[42] In total, over 712 of these planes were produced, but a number of them fell into the hands of the later Islamic Republic of Iran following the 1979 Islamic Revolution.

4

LONG ISLAND'S RACE TO THE MOON

On October 4, 1957, the Soviet Union launched the first satellite, *Sputnik*, into orbit. This successful launch spurred the collective imaginations of the world, but overall, it took the Cold War into a new unimaginable front. In response, the United States quickly assembled a launch for a satellite called *Vanguard Test Vehicle Three*. With high hopes, on December 6, 1957, the launch failed, as the rocket exploded seconds into the flight. The failed launch and Soviet success generated a fear that the United States was falling behind in space advancements. This quickly evolved into a crisis of confidence for American space engineering. In response, President Dwight D. Eisenhower proposed and signed into law the National Aeronautics and Space Act on July 29, 1958. This legislation created the National Aeronautics and Space Administration (NASA). The United States was further challenged by the Soviets during the American National Exhibition in Moscow. During this exhibition, debates flared as to which country had the best technological advancements. This public debate over which country held the cutting-edge innovation for the future became known as the Kitchen Debates. As Vice President Richard Nixon boasted about America's quality of life, Nikita Khrushchev rebutted:

"This is what America is capable of, and how long has she existed—300 years, 150 years of independence, and this is her level? We haven't quite reached 42 years, and in another 7 years, we'll be at the level of America, and after that, we'll go farther. As we pass you by, we'll wave "hi" to you,

and then, if you want, we'll stop and say, "Please come along behind us.... We've passed you by and in the technology."[43]

With the formation of NASA and the election of John F. Kennedy, the United States was still falling behind. On April 12, 1961, the Soviets sent Yuri Alekseyevich Gargarin into orbit, and he became the first human in space. In response to this latest blow, Kennedy declared the United States would put a man on the moon by the end of the decade. Following this declaration, Long Island had very little knowledge that nine thousand residents would work, day in and day out to keep Kennedy's promise and beat back the advancing Soviets.

In September 1962, eight firms sent bids in to design a spacecraft for the new Apollo program. The first challenge was the requirement to keep within a budget of $500 million. With these funds, the firm was to create a lunar taxi that would carry a three-man crew to the lunar surface and return them to the ship; the firm was also to design an additional vehicle known as the lunar excursion module (LEM).[44] The two frontrunners for this contract were Republic Aviation and Grumman. Within a month of the initial bid, Grumman was given the contract. Nassau county executive Eugene Nickerson, in a press conference, stated that this contract would bring "$1 billion to just under $2 billion in additional contractor work and have Grumman add several thousand more employees to their current fifteen thousand workforce, by close of the decade.…This is not a contract dependent on defense needs but one that is only by the minds of men."[45] With the contract awarded, Grumman set out to find a subcontractors for the radio devices on the module. In an effort to pull some of the money and jobs away from the Long Island region, Senator Ted Kennedy of Massachusetts personally visited Grumman and requested to shift some of the radio work to the Boston-based Radio Corp of America. In response, Suffolk County executive H. Lee Dennison demanded, "We have nothing to give away. Anything we get is going to stay right here."[46] But despite Dennison and other local elected officials protesting, Senator Kennedy managed to get the subcontracting work for his state.

Grumman selected Lockheed Martin engineer Thomas Kelly to head the lunar project. Kelly grew up in Merrick and previously worked in Grumman in the early 1950s. His engineering skills on the F11 Tiger propulsion systems made him well known, but he left to work on a missile program with Lockheed Martin. His professional success in developing missile systems and cutting-edge fighting planes was overshadowed by Kelly's strong desire to be part of the space program. While in Grumman during his first returning year, he developed the orbiting astronomical observatory (OAO). The OAO would later become the foundation for the *Hubble* space telescope. When expanding into a team, Kelly would later reflect, "We just pretty much let our imaginations run wild and let the form follow the function. It just kind of evolved. You basically started out with the two astronauts, and you had to wrap everything around them or design everything so that they could get at it and use it."[47] Leading a team under Kelly's leadership, a number of possible test vehicles were created that cost $400 million. All models were designed around a lunar orbit rendezvous method. This process was a three-part design that included a control center, a separate service module and a lunar lander. Once in orbit, crew members would go into the lunar lander. On the moon and after exploration, the upper portion of the lander would dock with the command module, and on the return to Earth, the service module would separate from the command module and crash back to Earth at an estimated twenty-five thousand miles per hour. The success of this operation depended on correct assumptions of what challenges the surface of the moon would have on any craft or person. The engineers anticipated the craft would need to be designed for heavy dust or layers of ice. Following the development of various test vehicles, Grumman was awarded an additional $1.19 billion to produce fifteen flight modules. This additional contract became the largest space and defense award ever in Long Island and American history prior to 1966.[48]

Advising the Grumman engineers was NASA's chief engineer Wernher von Braun. Von Braun, who was a Nazi war criminal, was brought to the United States after World War II in Operation Paperclip. Von Braun was most well-known for his work with the Nazi V1 and V2—"V" for *vengeance*—rockets and his use of slave labor in the development of his rockets with full knowledge of the Nazi's concentration camps. Further implicating him in the genocide was his rank of *sturmbannfuher* (major) in the Nazi SS. Despite his position and role in the Nazi SS, he was never held accountable for his use of slave labor or his role in the Holocaust. When Von Braun was confronted with his role in the Holocaust, he stated, "We wouldn't have treated your atomic scientists as war criminals, and I do not expect to be treated as one."[49] Making a deal with the devil, the United States rebranded his image as a skilled engineer who was going to take the country to the finish line in the space race. Before his work with Grumman, Von Braun was brought to Huntsville, Alabama's Redstone Arsenal to help develop a rocket similar to the V2. These rockets would

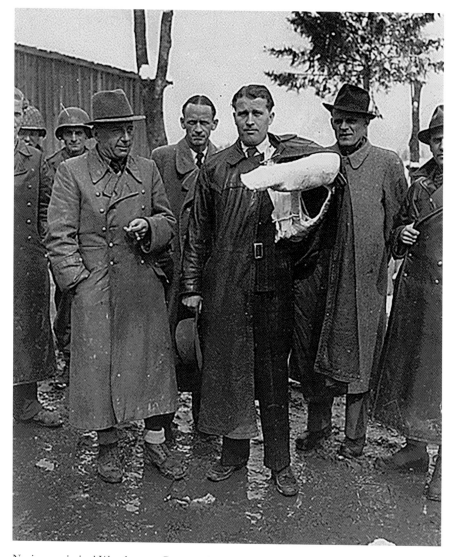

Nazi war criminal Wernher von Braun, who was arrested by U.S. forces in Europe following the German surrender. *Courtesy of the Library of Congress, Image Collection.*

originally be designed to carry nuclear warheads, and they were later redesigned to carry astronauts into orbit in 1961.

In Bethpage, Grumman's final construction of the modules was done within a clean room that was dust-free. All engineers and laborers had to put on smocks and have their shoes cleaned in a machine before entering the room. While perfecting the prototypes, challenges included providing a

Wernher von Braun, once captured, was brought over to United States in Operation Paper Clip. His first assignment as a NASA employee was to design rockets. *Courtesy of the Library of Congress, Image Collection.*

lightweight module, as every pound in orbit was estimated to weigh three pounds. With the weight figured into the module, a durable lightweight thermal shield had to be constructed. The solution was to wrap the module in a thin multilayered aluminized mylar cover that, in a vacuum, operated like a jacket filled in with multilayer insulation blankets. It had a combination of meteoroid protection and thermal shielding and was very lightweight.[50] More weight reduction was done with a chemical milling process that brought down the thickness of the metal while retaining the needed strength. The initial construction of the rockets had the assistance of Von Braun in the Grumman facility, but the final construction, tests and modification were done at Marshall Space Center in Huntsville, Alabama. Following years of innovation and billions of dollars, the first flight in Cape Kennedy, Florida, was scheduled for January 1968. Two hours before the final countdown of the first test flight, trouble developed with the freon gas system that was designed to cool the life support equipment.[51] Following troubleshooting, the module was launched. The fifth module flight was the iconic July 16–24, 1969 moon landing that established the United States' supremacy over the Soviets in space.

Following the success of the module, Grumman got to work completing the lunar rover. This project was pushed through by Von Braun. Head engineer Edward Markow, in 1965, patented the resilient wheel. This wheel was to work as a cleat with flexible spokes on the moon's surface. The rover was constructed in the Bethpage facility, but there were challenges to testing its effectiveness on the moon's surfaces. For testing, the engineers picked Long Island beaches, believing they would be the perfect simulation of the moon's surface, but after further studies, it was decided a rockier terrain was needed. The destination for the final tests was Pasadena, California. Before

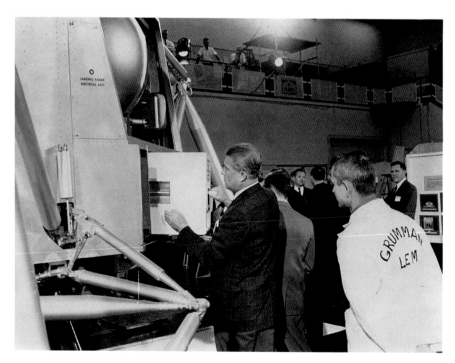

Wernher von Braun advised Grumman on their work with the lunar module. Pictured is Von Braun at Bethpage Grumman, inspecting the module. *Courtesy of the Cradle of Aviation.*

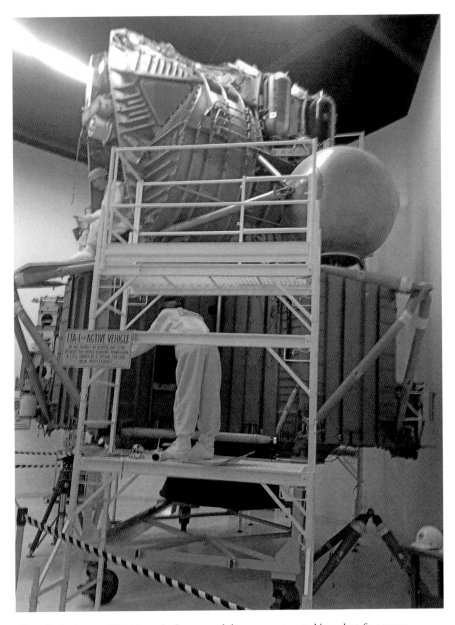

Above: A display model of how the lunar module was constructed in a dust-free room. *Courtesy of Christopher Verga.*

Opposite: A photograph of the finished lunar module. *Courtesy of NASA, Image Collection.*

being shipped off, the rover was sent through a demo run at the Calverton facility. At the test, Von Braun, who was on a routine visit, drove the vehicle around the runways to check its handling.[52] After several tests and NASA's evaluation of the competing prototypes from Boeing and General Motors, the Boeing lunar rover was selected for the Apollo 15 flight in 1971.

With the success of the module's operations in the Apollo program, Grumman expanded its experimentation and marketing of satellites. The OAO-2 (Orbiting Astronomical Observatory) was successfully launched into orbit in 1968 with eleven telescopes enclosed. While orbiting more than seventeen thousand times, the OAO-2 compiled data on the discovery of new comets, the heat and composition of stars and potential undiscovered galaxies and observed the process of a novae. The OAO-2 recorded data until it failed in 1973. Grumman began the construction of the OAO-3, commonly referred to as the *Copernicus* satellite, which conducted more advanced operations. Launched in 1972, the satellite was equipped to provide data for an ultraviolet star study at Princeton University and carry

X-ray experiment for the University College London. The *Copernicus* stayed operational until 1981. The third satellite Grumman experimented with in the early 1970s was the large space telescope (LST). The LST was an attempt to make the OAO obsolete. The LST was designed with a three-meter-long optical system that would include a solar power station.

In an effort to recapture some additional space exploration contracts, Grumman and Boeing teamed up to design a reusable shuttle that would be launched using unmanned boosters. The concept shuttle was to be marketed for short-term travel, such as satellite repair or other orbital missions.[53] Unfortunately, this design remained a concept model and never made it to production or received a NASA contract. The success of the Grumman's space program did not carry the company through the 1970s. Grumman's total net sales in 1969 were $1,180,328,000, but in 1970, they dropped to $993,260,754 and fell by almost $200 million in 1971 to $799,021,180. The decreased revenues made Grumman shrink its space program, and many of its engineers were lost to competitors.

As Grumman was losing its footing with NASA contracts, Republic Fairchild was getting a second lease on its test for innovation. The Space Shuttle Enterprise construction had a large portion of its contract awarded to Republic in 1975. The *Enterprise* would be the project's first orbiter, and it was a reusable part of the shuttle reentry. The orbit stabilizers and fuselages would be made in the Farmingdale plant. The construction of the components would keep Republic economically strong until 1976. The launch the *Enterprise* was a success, and the components were delivered on time, but despite all the good results, Republic would not have a NASA contract renewed. Today, the *Enterprise* is on display at the Intrepid Aircraft Carrier Museum in New York City. The last flight of the *Enterprise* was launched on April 27, 2012; it was a final tour with all components still functional as they were in the first test flight of 1976.

5

SECRET WEAPONS AND HUMAN EXPERIMENTS

During the Cold War, Long Island became the home of U.S. government laboratories, tucked into the outskirts of the suburban metropolis.

Brookhaven National Laboratory and Plum Island Animal Disease Center become the center of many stories—from secret documentation of radiation effects on humans to fostering a potentially deadly biological weapon that would cause the destruction of a food supply.

For decades, these stories were shared among locals around family dinner tables and backroom bars. But these stories as science fiction sounding as they are, have truths, and become part of Long Island's narrative.

Brookhaven National Laboratory

It was a letter from Long Island that led to the development of nuclear weapons—which were central to the Cold War. Addressed to President Franklin D. Roosevelt and signed by Albert Einstein, it was sent from Peconic in August 1939. Einstein rented a vacation cottage on Old Grove Road on Nassau Point in Peconic.

The letter, which fellow physicist Leo Szilard had a major part in crafting, followed meetings at Einstein's summer retreat that included Szilard, Enrico Fermi and Edward Teller. Fission—the splitting of the atom—had been accomplished using uranium in late 1938 in Berlin. And the scientists, all of whom had sought refuge in the United States with the rise of Hitler in Germany, feared that the process "could be used by the Nazis to build devastating weaponry."[54]

The letter went on to explain:

> *Some recent work by E. Fermi and L. Szilard, which has been communicated to me in manuscripts, leads me to expect that the element uranium may be turned into a new and important source of energy in the immediate future. Certain aspects of the situation which has arisen seem to call for watchfulness and, if necessary, quick action on the part of the administration. I believe, therefore, that it is my duty to bring to your attention the following facts and recommendations.*

It continued:

> *It may become possible to set up a nuclear chain reaction in a large mass of uranium by which vast amounts of power and large quantities of new radium-like elements would be generated. Now, it appears almost certain that this could be achieved in the immediate future. This phenomenon would also lead to the construction of bombs, and it is conceivable—though much less certain—that extremely powerful bombs of a new type may thus be constructed. A single bomb of this type, carried by boat and exploded in a port, might very well destroy the whole port together with some of the surrounding territory. However, such bombs might very well prove to be too heavy for transportation by air. In view of this situation, you may think it desirable to have some permanent contact maintained between the administration and the group of physicists working on chain reactions in America....One possible way of achieving this might be for you to entrust with this task a person who has your confidence* [who would] *approach government departments, keep them informed of the further development and put forward recommendations for government action, giving particular attention to the problem of securing a supply of uranium ore for the United States.* [Also, this person would endeavor] *to speed up the experimental work, which is, at present, being carried on within the limits of the budgets of university laboratories, by providing funds, if such funds be required, through his contacts with private persons who are willing to make contributions for this cause, and perhaps also by obtaining the co-operation of industrial laboratories which have the necessary equipment. I understand that Germany has actually stopped the sale of uranium from the Czechoslovakian mines, which she has taken over.*[55]

This letter of concern led to the creation of the Manhattan Project, the crash program during World War II to produce nuclear weapons—to beat Germany to the production of atomic weaponry.

In the end, Einstein regretted signing the letter. "If I had known that the Germans would not succeed in constructing the atom bomb, I never would have moved a finger," he declared in his 1946 book, *Out of My Later Years.* The Manhattan Project involved laboratories and manufacturing plants set up all over the United States, the largest ones being located in Los Alamos, New Mexico; Argonne, Illinois; and Oak Ridge, Tennessee.

In August 1945, atomic bombs built by the Manhattan Project were dropped on Hiroshima and Nagasaki, Japan. Then, with the end of World War II, there was anxiety among those involved in the Manhattan Project about what was next for them. As James Kunetka wrote in his book *City of Fire* about the Los Alamos laboratory, with the war over, there were then the problems of "job placement, work continuity…more free time than work." There was "hardly enough to keep everyone busy.…Without a crash program underway, the laboratory found itself, for the first time, discouraging overtime, and staff members and their families were encouraged to take accumulated leaves."[56]

But some of the people and corporations involved—including Westinghouse and General Electric—were major government contractors for the Manhattan Project and sought additional work involving nuclear technology. More atomic bombs were manufactured and stockpiled. But what else could be done with nuclear technology to perpetuate the vested nuclear interest of the Manhattan Project?

There were studies made within the Manhattan Project as the war ended to figure out how the project's activities could be extended. Two committees were established: one headed by Zay Jeffries, a General Electric executive, and another led by Richard C. Tolman, a science advisor to General Leslie Groves, the head of the Manhattan Project. Both urged the development of scientific and industrial applications of nuclear technology.

The political vehicle that permitted the activities of the Manhattan Project to go on was the Atomic Energy Act of 1946, which created the Atomic Energy Commission (AEC). On December 31 of that year, it took over the Manhattan's Project's facilities and its personnel.

A new laboratory was also proposed that would focus on atomic research and the development of civilian uses for nuclear technology. This was to be the AEC's Brookhaven National Laboratory (BNL), located on an eight-mile-square former army base called Camp Upton in Upton, Long Island.

Above: The entrance of Brookhaven National Laboratory, first opened under the Atomic Energy Commission. *Courtesy of the Brookhaven National Laboratory.*

Opposite, top: The first scientific colloquium at Brookhaven in 1947. Physics Department chairman Norman Ramsey (*front, second from left*). *Courtesy of the Brookhaven National Laboratory.*

Opposite, bottom: The graphite reactor, constructed in 1947, remained operational until the late 1990s. *Courtesy of the Brookhaven National Laboratory.*

Under the direction of the Atomic Energy Commission, a graphite reactor was constructed in 1947 and was in operation from 1950 to 1968. BNL was managed from its outset in 1947 until 1998 by Associated Universities, a combination of nine universities, including Harvard, Yale, Princeton and the Massachusetts Institute of Technology. Associated Universities was fired, however, in 1998, after there was a disclosure that the largest nuclear facility constructed and operated there, the High Flux Beam Reactor, had, for years, been leaking radioactive tritium into the groundwater below. Long Island is dependent on an underground water table as its sole source of potable water. The BNL's management contract was subsequently given to Stony Brook University and Ohio-based Battelle Memorial Institute. In addition to its reactors, BNL would develop a particle accelerator, but the main focus of the lab was atomic energy and technology.

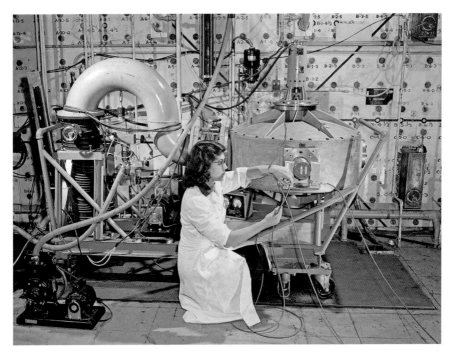

Women researchers working on a neutron chopper in the graphite reactor in the mid-1950s. *Courtesy of the Brookhaven National Laboratory.*

The construction of the high-flux beam reactor in 1965. *Courtesy of the Brookhaven National Laboratory.*

This page: Scientists working on the bubble chamber. This was a physics experiment that heated electrically charged particles. *Courtesy of the Brookhaven National Laboratory.*

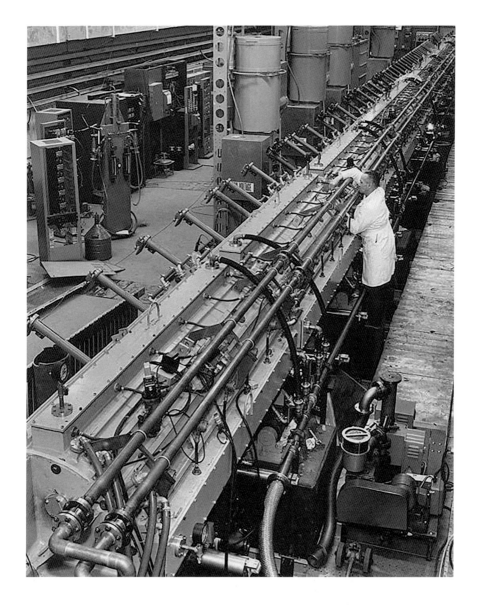

A major Cold War activity of BNL involved it being in charge of monitoring the radiation effects among the people of the Marshall Islands as the United States developed even more powerful nuclear weapons— mightier atomic bombs and the hydrogen bomb—and tested them in the waters around the Marshall Islands. With over sixty-eight bombs tested by the end of the 1950s, thousands of Marshallese became refugees. With many refugees fleeing the islands, BNL scientists took advantage of the

Opposite: The first linear/ particle accelerator, 1952. Used for the study of condensed matter. *Courtesy of the Brookhaven National Laboratory.*

Left: Head of the ion collider project, Satoshi Ozaki, sitting next to the magnet of the collider in 1994. *Courtesy of the Brookhaven National Laboratory.*

Below: Delivery of the ion collider, which was designed to study the creation of the universe through the collision of particles. *Courtesy of the Brookhaven National Laboratory.*

contaminated land mass by convincing islanders to return to their string of islands contaminated with radioactivity.

In 1988, the Marshall Islands Nuclear Claims Tribunal was established to study the damage of nuclear testing and the negligence of Brookhaven Lab scientists and doctors. The estimated damages to the Marshallese would total $1 billion, and the tribunal exposed a disturbing history of human experimentation. As *Newsday* reported in an extensive 2009 exposé by reporter Thomas Maier, headlined "Cold War Fallout for Brookhaven National Lab,": "In 2007, the Marshall Islands Nuclear Claims Tribunal… determined Rongelap's residents had been ill-served by the [BNL] doctors.… [And] the doctors' primary responsibility to address medical concerns had been trumped by the goal of studying the effects of nuclear radiation on the human body."

The islanders declared to the tribunal that they "came to feel like guinea pigs, used for experimentation by the U.S." having the islanders continue to live on contaminated islands "supported scientific research and military defense concerns."

The tribunal stated it found "that the BNL doctors returned the residents to Rongelap…after a three-year absence, even though they knew it was highly contaminated.…BNL used their return as a chance to study the flow of radioactive toxins through the body."

Long Island journalist Karl Grossman interviewed Glenn Alcalay, who was a witness to the events while serving as a Peace Corps volunteer between 1975 and 1977 on the Marshall Islands. Alcalay told Grossman that he was appalled by what he had seen—"a secretive human radiation experiment before my eyes," with a "key role played" by Brookhaven National Laboratory. Alcalay further elaborated, "I saw firsthand the lingering and insidious effects of radioactive fallout among the people of Utrick Atoll [where he served in the Peace Corps]. I witnessed six health surveys sponsored by Brookhaven National Laboratory under the auspices of the Department of Energy. It did not take much insight to realize that the Brookhaven program was fraught with a myriad number of severe shortcomings, including a nearly total lack of sensitivity for Marshallese culture and habits."[57] In a New York AEC meeting in 1956, prior to the start of the experiment, various Brookhaven doctors agreed that "Data of this type has never been available. While it is true that these people do not live the way westerners do, civilized people, it is nonetheless also true that they are more like us than the mice." Further documented evidence was found in a 1958 annual report written by Dr. Robert Conard of the

Brookhaven/AEC medical surveillance team. The report stated, "The habitation of these people on Rongelap Island afford the opportunity for a most valuable ecological radiation study on human beings….The various radionuclides present on the island can be traced from the soil through the food chain and into the human being." With the eyewitness accounts, meeting minutes and annual reports, it was clear that the scientists exposed the locals to contamination willingly in an effort to study the effects of it, even with the understanding that the side effects could be lethal.

With the annual reports and the meeting minutes in hand, Alcalay, on behalf of the Nuclear-Free Pacific Network, was called to provide testimony in 1984 to the subcommittee of the Committee on Appropriations of the U.S. House of Representatives. Prior to the testimony, Alcalay interviewed the locals of the islands who were eyewitness to the bomb testing and human studies. Marshallese witnesses and victims provided written statements that included interviews Alcalay had conducted with Marshallese in 1981, in which they told of their presence during the nuclear detonations and the after effects. One witness, Nina Latobe, recalled:

> *I was inside my house at the time of "the bomb," i.e. the Bravo hydrogen bomb test of March 1, 1954, and when I came out, I saw the red light in the western sky, and then I heard the loud explosion. Shortly afterwards, I felt much fatigue and also felt nauseous.* [Three months afterward,] *some women gave birth to creatures that looked more like cats, rats, and the insides of turtles—maybe like intestines. Most of the women had "jibun" (miscarriages), including myself, who gave birth to something that was not like a human being. Some women gave birth to things resembling grapes and other fruits, and some women even stopped having children, including me. Things are not the same now, and people are not as active and healthy as they were before "the bomb." The DOE (Department of Energy) doctors try to reassure us, but even now, I am nauseous and tired most of the time, and I know this is from "the bomb." The DOE doctors try to tell us that this is normal for people all over the world and that it is not related to the "poison." Now, I believe that the "poison" will not go away from our island. The DOE doctors treat us as if we were animals for their use, and they do not tell us the truth about our problems. Could you please help us to find honest doctors to tell us the truth about our sicknesses? I also believe that all of the Marshall Islands have "poison," and I believe that the DOE doctors have been keeping secrets from us for many years about our condition.*[58]

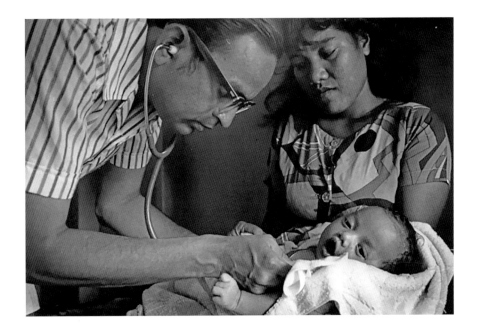

This page: A Brookhaven National Laboratory–based medical team documenting the effects of being exposed to radiation from various detonations of atomic and hydrogen bombs on the Marshallese people in the mid-1950s. *Courtesy of the United States Department of Energy.*

In 2002, Alcalay submitted, at the request of the Utrik Atoll local government and the Office of the Public Advocate involved in the Marshall Island Nuclear Claims Tribunal, a report titled *Living in a Utrik Atoll: The Sociocultural Impact Radioactive Environment.* It began, "As a Peace Corps volunteer on Utrik Atoll between May 1975 and May 1977, I learned firsthand from the people of Utrik about their continuing problems associated with living in a radioactively contaminated environment." The Alcalay report included interviews he had conducted in 1981 with residents of Utrik, which included highly critical comments about Brookhaven National Laboratory's activities on the Marshall Islands. In this report, Arta Rijon said, "The United States tested bombs in our islands because they view the Marsallese as animals for their studies....Dr. Conard has little sympathy for our problems, and we now need truly independent doctors to help us with our sicknesses....I believe [the BNL doctors] came to study us, not to help us."[59] And Alden Matthew stated, "The first thing I would say is that the DOE doctors have never told us the truth and that we don't trust the doctors. They come and study us like animals in an experiment."

In the report's conclusion, Alcalay decried the "inherent conflict of interest in having the same agencies that help develop and test nuclear weapons doing the follow-up medical and scientific studies," leading to "a historic trend to downplay the effects of radiation." The $1 billion settlement could not repair the damages to the natives' homeland, the high cancer rates, and birth deformities.

IN THE EARLY 1970s, BNL was in the middle of the push by the Long Island Lighting Company to extend nuclear technology to the island—to build seven to eleven nuclear power plants on the 120-mile-square slender land mass east of Manhattan. Phyllis Vineyard, the wife of BNL director George Vineyard, was a paid member of the LILCO board of directors beginning in 1974, and from 1987 to 1994, she was the customer services consultant to LILCO chairman and CEO William Catacosinos, the former assistant director of BNL.[60] Not only did Vineyard and Catacosinos push for nuclear power on Long Island, but many of the scientists and engineers at BNL were enmeshed in the drive, too. They formed Suffolk Scientists for a Cleaner Environment and Safer Energy, which lobbied for the nuclear push. The BNL scientists and engineers also served as expert witnesses at federal and state hearings on LILCO's Shoreham nuclear power plant project and also served as expert witnesses at hearings on LILCO's bid to build four nuclear plants along the Long Island Sound east of Shoreham at Jamesport.

The abandonment of a nuclear power plant along the East River in Ravenswood, Queens, by Consolidated Edison (ConEd), the electric utility company based in Manhattan, opened the door to the LILCO nuclear push. The one-thousand-megawatt plant of Westinghouse design was to be located north of the Queensboro Bridge across from midtown Manhattan. Stiff citizen opposition led the New York City Council, in 1963, to propose a law banning the siting of a nuclear plant within the city. As the June 15, 1963 daily *Long Island Press* editorialized: "Considering that the Ravenswood site is almost smack in the geographic center of New York City, with its teeming millions...opposition to it is understandable, to say the least." There were officials of the U.S. Atomic Energy Commission open to siting nuclear power plants in cities. Several presented their view at "a session of the Nuclear Energy Writers Association" that there could be "engineered safeguards," just as, in 1963, ConEd canceled the project. "No Atoms for Peace in Queens" was the headline in the January 7, 1964, *New York Herald Tribune.*

However, others at the AEC were concerned about locating nuclear plants in cities, preferring instead areas of lower population. LILCO's service area, although having a far denser population than most areas of the United States, was less highly populated than New York City. Still, Long Island is the most populous island in the United States. Also, with nuclear plants needing a massive amount of cooling water to operate—a plant of one thousand megawatts requiring one million gallons of water a minute—Long Island was promoted by LILCO as being well-suited for the string of nuclear power plants the company sought to build to provide nuclear-generated electricity for Long Island and the Northeast.

But LILCO had a record of dismal mismanagement. In the 1930s and 1940s, it was regularly on the ropes. "You heard about LILCO being in tremendous difficulty, ready to go belly up," said Anne Mead, a Long Island attorney and a member of the New York State Public Service Commission. That commission, in its 1948 annual report, declared that the common stocks of LILCO "have no value [and] are not backed by assets. Indeed, in that year, ConEd filed a petition with the commission to acquire control of the troubled utility, but in 1950, it decided against it.[61]

LILCO, as it launched its nuclear drive, stressed its mutually advantageous link with BNL in a booklet titled *Atomic Power for Long Island*, which was distributed at a press conference in April 1966 where it announced the

Shoreham project. The plans for Atomic Power for Long Island and building the relationship between BNL were in works for over a decade prior to the LILCO nuclear drive.

> *One winter day in 1953, two LILCO engineers drove out to Brookhaven National Laboratory to attend the first of what turned out to be a year-long series of weekly lectures on reactor design principles and related topics. The lectures were held on Wednesdays, and it was not long before the attendees became known around the laboratory as "Wednesday Boys."[62] The association with the Brookhaven staff proved to be of mutual advantage. There was much to learn and the atmosphere at the laboratory was a stimulating one. In return, LILCO engineers brought a fresh point of view to bear on many difficult engineering problems with which the laboratory was then dealing in the reactor field. On completion of the lecture course, we sent a man to work full time at Brookhaven—an arrangement we maintained for five years—and over the years have continued to keep in close touch with the laboratory's reactor activities.[63]*

This established relationship paved the way for LILCO's plan for Shoreham, referred to as Shoreham Unit 1 in LILCO licensing papers, which was to then build Shoreham 2 and a Shoreham 3 nuclear power plants on the same site.

Getting utilities in the United States interested in nuclear power was part of the original mission of BNL, to promote civilian uses of nuclear technology. With its linkage to LILCO, BNL was working intimately with its at-home electric utility. As Tom Twomey, an attorney for the opposition to the multinuclear power plant plan, said, LILCO wanted Long Island to become a "nuclear park," the AEC term at the time for areas in the United States where nuclear plants would be concentrated. The AEC construction permit hearings for Shoreham turned out to be a forum on nuclear power, and they laid the foundations for later, wide-scale public opposition to LILCO's nuclear program. The conclusion of the hearings was foregone: the AEC, set up to both promote and regulate nuclear power, never denied a construction or operating permit for a nuclear power plant. Attorney Irving Like noted that the panel's chairman was Jack Campbell, "the former governor of New Mexico—known as the playground of the AEC and nuclear industry for its extensive uranium mining and milling, Los Alamos Laboratory, other nuclear facilities and an overall close relationship with nuclear technology—and two technical members connected to the national nuclear laboratories." But attorney Like, who was to be highly active for decades in antinuclear power opposition on Long Island, embraced a strategy of: "If you can't beat them, you can, at least, expose them."[64] Conducted between 1970 and 1972, the hearings turned into a landmark trial for nuclear power—an outcome not expected by LILCO or BNL. "Even though a lot of people woke up after Three Mile Island," said Richard Pollack, the former head of Critical Mass, formed by Ralph Nader to challenge atomic energy, "we regard Shoreham as the real beginning."[65] The hearings were the longest proceedings ever held in the United States for a nuclear plant licensing case.

A central issue: accidents and their consequences. This included loss-of-coolant core meltdown accidents. Nearly a decade before the core meltdown, the formation of a hydrogen bubble and the concern that it would explode at the Three Mile Island nuclear power plant in Pennsylvania in 1979, there were many hours of testimony dealing with the probability of these accidents. This was three decades before the three Fukushima nuclear power plants in Japan formed hydrogen bubbles, which did explode as all three underwent loss-of-coolant core meltdowns in 2011. (The Shoreham nuclear power plant was the same type of General Electric Mark I reactor as the reactors that had meltdowns resulting in hydrogen explosions at Fukushima.) Moreover, fifteen years before the Chernobyl nuclear plant erupted in an explosion, there was extensive testimony at the Shoreham hearing on the "nuclear runaway" or "power excursion" accident and its potential to cause a massive explosion. Attorney Like introduced the problem of evacuating usually traffic-clogged Long Island in case of a major Shoreham accident. But the chairman of the AEC panel refused that this issue could only be considered when it came time to consider granting an operating license for Shoreham. Like insisted that the panel abide by the 1970 National Environmental Policy Act (NEPA) that required agencies of the federal government to consider all environmental aspects of and alternatives to a project before approving it. The panel refused, but after the U.S. Second District Court of appeals ruled that the AEC had to consider NEPA in a case involving the Calvert Cliffs Nuclear Project in Maryland, the Shoreham hearings became the first forum on nuclear power to adhere to the act. Dr. Alice Stewart, the director of social medicine at Oxford University, came from England and told of her work that established children whose mothers received small amounts of radiation through X-rays during pregnancy—amounts thought not to be dangerous—ran twice the risk of developing leukemia than those whose

The war room. Local activists meeting to discuss the next steps in preventing the activation of the Shoreham Nuclear Power Plant. *Courtesy of the Irving Like Estate.*

mothers had not. She denied the AEC's claim of a "threshold dose," below which radiation would not cause cancer, stating that any amount of radiation could cause cancer.

Dr. Ernest Sternglass, a professor of radiation physics at the University of Pittsburgh School of Medicine, cited his research that showed increases in infant mortality in Suffolk County due to the operation of the High-Flux Beam Reactor at BNL. In response, Andrew Hull, the secretary of Suffolk Scientists for Cleaner Power and Safer Environment and a health physicist at BNL, insisted that the releases were within the limits set by the federal government.

The hearings focused on the first major U.S. study of the impacts of a nuclear power plant accident—which was done at BNL and released in 1957. The report, *Theoretical Possibilities and Consequences of Major Accidents in Large Nuclear Plants*, with AEC serial number WASH-740, estimated that a "worst case" accident at a 200-megawatt plant could result in 3,400 deaths and 43,000 injuries, with property damage as high as $7 billion. "People could be killed at distances up to 15 miles and injured at distances of about 45 miles. Land contamination could extend for greater distance," it stated. Likewise, an accident at Shoreham, an 820-megawatt plant, could release substantially more radioactivity and be far more lethal.[66] Lester L. Wolff, then a Long Island congressional representative, testified that Shoreham would "be a colossal gamble with the health of future genes" and said he did not approve of the AEC's procedure that resulted in it never turning down an application to run a nuclear plant.[67]

Indeed, Wolff's observation of the conduct of the licensing panel at the Shoreham hearings resulted in his leading an effort in Congress to abolish the AEC, which occurred in 1974. After two years, the hearings ended, and the AEC granted LILCO a permit to build Shoreham. The company had already spent $77 million on the plant, and there was a front-page photograph in *Newsday* on the day of the decision, April 12, 1973; the image showed the massive seventy-five-foot-tall steel frame of the reactor building. LILCO claimed it was simply "site preparation," and the AEC agreed. In the 1980s, amid intense public and governmental opposition to nuclear power on Long Island, Shoreham was prevented from going into commercial operation. With anxieties heightened by the Three Mile Island accident in 1979 and then the Shoreham Nuclear Power Plant construction documents that became public, the campaign suffered. Found at the Southold town dump by a person who was browsing for furniture to refinish, the documents were passed on to a newspaper photographer who brought them to Karl Grossman. All of the more than 1,000 reports from the Stone & Webster Engineering Corporation, the architect/manager of Shoreham's construction, involved problems in the plant's construction. In 416 of the reports, a box for "Nuclear Safety Related" problems was checked. Grossman worked with Dr. Michio Kaku, a professor of physics at the City University of New York, and MHB Technical Associates of California, whose three principals were former supervisors at General Electric, Shoreham reactor's manufacturer, in examining the documents.

In Kaku's opinion: "The attitude through the documents was one of "Let's just sand it smooth and pass it on." In his and MHB's judgment, the documents were replete with examples of below-standard construction that deviated from engineering specifications, with the consistent remedy that the specifications would thus be changed. "These documents make you jump up and down and ask, 'What are they doing?'" Kaku told Grossman in an interview.[68]

The "dump documents"—placed under a bush at the Southold dump in the weeks after the Three Mile Island accident—were an issue at the 1979 trial, the first of more than six hundred persons arrested at the Shoreham site and taken into custody on June 3, 1979, in a demonstration that drew fifteen thousand persons. It was one of many anti-Shoreham protests and

This page: Antinuclear activist and lawyer Irving Like presenting his case against the Shoreham Nuclear Power Plant. *Courtesy of the Irving Like Estate.*

was described in *Newsday* as the "largest demonstration in Long Island history."[69] Using the dump papers and testimony from several workers, the defense contended that the plant posed a threat to life, so there was "legal justification" for civil disobedience. One Shoreham worker, John Everett, testified that Shoreham "was not being built to specifications" and alleged the use of defective concrete. He testified that incorrect welding materials were used routinely, and when he told NRC inspectors about the poor construction, they "promptly" sabotaged any investigation and revealed him as a source. The case, tried, was titled *The People of the State of New York v. Matthew J. Chachere.* Other Shoreham whistleblowers subsequently came forward, including two former plant inspectors, George W. Henry and Ronald Stanchfield. They both testified at a special session of the Suffolk County legislature in 1985. Henry said during his testimony that if Shoreham was allowed to operate, "there is catastrophe ahead." Stanchfield, who had worked at six nuclear plants, testified to having "never seen incompetence en masse as goes on at Shoreham." Managers denied or sought to cover up problems, he said. "What has happened…is a crime.… And it sits there, belligerently threatening our very lives."[70] LILCO CEO and chairman and former BNL assistant director Catacosinos told a group of reporters at a meeting Grossman was present for that he would conduct "guerrilla warfare" to put the plant into operation. "Long Island needs Shoreham," he insisted. He said he was well familiar with nuclear power from his years at BNL and said that in case of an accident, radioactivity would simply go "up in the atmosphere."[71]

The NRC, in 1980, gave LILCO a license to construct two 1,150-megawatt Westinghouse nuclear power plants at Jamesport, but this was blocked by a New York Board on Electric Generation, Siting and the Environment, which had been created too late for Shoreham. The approval of this board was needed before a new plant could be built. LILCO planned to build four nuclear power plants at Jamesport.

Meanwhile, Suffolk County commissioned a study on the feasibility of evacuation in the event of a major Shoreham accident, a study that came to the conclusion—as Like had warned at the AEC construction permit hearings—that it could not be successful. Following the Three Mile Island accident, the Nuclear Regulatory Commission, a successor agency of the AEC, ruled that no nuclear plant could operate without an in-place emergency plan that could be implemented by state or local government. Based on that study, in 1983, Suffolk County refused to adopt an emergency plan, and Governor Mario Cuomo and New York State supported the conclusion that an evacuation was not possible. That was the key strategy against Shoreham in the early 1980s—an insistence that evacuation wasn't feasible, so the plant should not be allowed to open.

There was also the issue of constantly escalating cost. LILCO's 1966 press release announcing the Shoreham project estimated its cost to be "in the $65–75 million range." But by the time the plant's construction was over, the cost was calculated to be between $6.5–7.5 billion, a 10,000 percent cost overrun, making it, by far, the most expensive nuclear plant per proposed kilowatt of electricity ever built at the time.

There was intense pressure from Washington to have Shoreham open. "The Shoreham plant must open," declared U.S. Department of Energy secretary John S. Herrington at a Nuclear Power Assembly, a nuclear industry gathering in 1985. "If it doesn't, the signals will be a low point in this industry. If it does, we are going to begin a brand-new era."[72] LILCO, in 1985, began low-power testing of the plant. Many operating problems ensued. It was another strategy to stop Shoreham that culminated in a final victory. Like and his brother-in-law, Maurice Barbash, created Citizens to Replace LILCO. As a full-page advertisement that it ran in Long Island newspapers declared in 1986: "The problem isn't just whether Shoreham is safe, nor just whether thousands of men, women and children can get off Long Island quickly and safely in case of an accident…all legitimate fears. The real problem is LILCO."

In the push for nuclear technology after World War II, its promoters in the U.S. government had preempted states from being involved in many issues. But, Like—whose many credits include being an author of the New York State Conservation Bill of Rights, which became part of the state constitution in 1970—realized that what was not eliminated was under condemnation authority. This same power of condemnation, of eminent domain, that a government can use if, for example, a landowner will not sell property for the widening of a road, could be applied, Like determined, to block LILCO and stop Shoreham. The vehicle would be the creation of a state agency with condemnation power, a Long Island Power Authority (LIPA).

With the Citizens to Replace LILCO in the lead, a bill creating LIPA was passed by the New York State legislature and signed into law by Governor Mario Cuomo. That was the endgame. LILCO gave up. Shoreham was turned over to LIPA for a nominal one dollar and decommissioned as a nuclear facility.

All throughout the decades-long fight against Shoreham and nuclear power on Long Island, there were a variety of groups in the battle, among

The Shoreham Nuclear Power Plant today. It was constructed but never activated. *Courtesy of Christopher Verga.*

them were the Peoples Action Coalition, Shoreham Opponents Coalition, the SHAD Alliance and the Citizens Committee to Replace LILCO.

As attorney Twomey concluded:

> *LILCO wanted to convert its business from retailing on Long Island to wholesaling power throughout the entire Northeast—from Boston down to Washington—through commandeering the eastern portion of Long Island. I think LILCO has been saved from its own corporate insanity. I doubt they have any plans for nuclear power any longer, period—because of more than twenty-five years of blood, sweat and tears by thousands of average citizens who used their own common sense to conclude that nuclear power made no economic sense.*[73]

As the *Nation* magazine summed up in an editorially headed article, "As Shoreham Goes":

> *If people organize and fight back, they can win, even against the formidable forces that backed Shoreham.... The kind of dedicated, consistent, focused and massive grassroots effort brought against Shoreham on Long Island, which stressed political action, civil disobedience and public education on nuclear power, can and should be duplicated elsewhere in the United States to prevent the opening of nuclear plants now under construction and to shut down the potential Chernobyls among us.*[74]

In the end, still hanging on, the last to give up in the fight for the Shoreham nuclear power plant were the Brookhaven National Laboratory scientists and engineers, who, in a last-ditch effort, filed a lawsuit in U.S. District Court to try to prevent the end of Shoreham. They failed. And then, a few years later, their polluting reactors at BNL were shut down; at the lead of this fight was yet another Long Island grassroots organization, Standing for Truth About Radiation. This was the start of making Long Island nuclear free.

PLUM ISLAND

Over a century ago, the federal government purchased Plum Island, and in the late 1890s, it built Fort Terry, which served as a coastal artillery post for the United States military. The 840-acre island, a mile and a half off Orient Point at the eastern tip of Long Island's North Fork, is in a strategic location: the Atlantic entrance to the Long Island Sound. A maze of trenches was dug, and guns were placed in them, ready to fire at enemy ships that were feared to be heading west to attack New York City during the Spanish-American War. This mission of shelling enemy ships continued through World War I and World War II. But after World War II, with bombers in the sky rather than ships in the water regarded as the more likely instruments in a wartime attack on the largest city in the United States, the guns were removed. The trenches, however, remained.

Suffolk County reached out to the War Assets Administration in 1948 to acquire the island but was rebuffed by the federal government. In April that year, the U.S. Congress passed Public Law 48-496, which ostensibly established a new framework for Plum Island. It stated: "The secretary of

An aerial photograph of the Plum Island Animal Disease Center. *Courtesy of the United States Department of Agriculture.*

The Plum Island Coast Guard Base in 1951, before the 1954 opening of the Animal Disease Center. *Courtesy of the United States Department of Agriculture.*

agriculture is authorized to establish research laboratories…for research and study…of hoof-and-mouth disease and other animal disease."

There was local opposition from the North Fork to siting such a facility on Plum Island. The Greenport Oyster Growers Protective Association maintained that pollution from sewage generated from such an operation would contaminate the oyster beds. The head of the association, George Vanderborgh, stated, "The proposed facility will be the end of a $6 million industry. It will throw hundreds out of work and destroy the reputation of the Long Island oyster throughout the world."[75] North Fork dairy farmers rallied against having an animal disease laboratory on Plum Island. They demanded that Congressman Ernest Greenwood, whose First Congressional District encompassed the area, intervene. But in response to Greenwood's call to have construction of a laboratory on Plum Island slowed until further studies were conducted, Department of Agriculture officials assured the opponents that the laboratory would have no windows and that laboratory materials—and the bodies of animals experimented on—would be incinerated to reduce the potential spread of pathogens.

The opponents didn't know half of it. In 1952, at the same time Plum Island was in the process of being selected for the site of an animal disease facility, the U.S. Army was awarding a construction contract for what would be a center for biological warfare on Plum Island. This warfare would be directed against an enemy's animal food supply.[76] It took four decades for the truth to be revealed. "PLUM ISLAND'S Shadowy Past, Once-Secret Documents: Lab's Mission was Germ Warfare," declared the headline in *Newsday* on November 21, 1983, blowing the whistle journalistically on what had been established on Plum Island years before. The lead paragraph of the article by *Newsday* investigative reporter John McDonald stated: "A 1950s military plan to cripple the Soviet economy by killing horses, cattle and swine called for making biological warfare weapons out of exotic animal diseases at a Plum Island laboratory, now declassified army records reveal."[77] It continued, "Documents and interviews disclose for the first time what officials have denied for years: that the mysterious and closely guarded animal lab off the East End of Long Island was originally designed to conduct top-secret research into replicating dangerous viruses that could be used to destroy enemy livestock." The multipage article said "officials who run the Plum Island Animal Disease Center have long denied any involvement in biological warfare research and say their work is restricted to experiments designed to protect the nation's livestock from potentially fatal plagues."[78] It went on, "But military documents once stamped SECRET and recently obtained by *Newsday* from the Army Chemical and Biological Defense Agency shed light on the thinking of an earlier era, describing in unusually candiad langage the need to construct a laboratory on Plum Island for offensive germ warfare." The piece quoted one of the U.S. Army documents *Newsday* obtained, using the U.S. Freedom of Information Act, as stating: "The Operations Research Office has made a comprehensive study of offensive potentiallity of anti-animal agents. The report emphasize the importance of livestock in the economy of the USSR and the probable feasibility of attack. The U.S. Air Force has established a firm requirement for offensive munitions and agents for use against horses, cattle and swine."[79]

If there was any question about the veracity of the piece, *Newsday* covered its front page with a facsimile of a portion of one of the army documents. The front page was emblazoned with the document and its words: "PLUM ISLAND will permit the Chemical Corps to executive required projects in connecion with imported agents...and others that might become of BW [biological warfare] significance." And *Newsday* added as the source: "From a declassified 1951 document."

The Plum Island Animal Disease Laboratory, aerial photograph. *Courtesy of the United States Department of Agriculture.*

In 2004, Michael Carroll, utilizing his skills as an attorney, further "connected the dots" on the Plum Island Cold War story with publication of his book *Lab 257: The Story of the Government's Secret Plum Island Germ Laboratory.* It became a national best-seller. Carroll's research over seven years included six trips to Plum Island until, as he notes in *Lab 257*, "I was abrupty denied further access...on the grounds of 'national security.'" Carroll interviewed numerous people, including "current and former scientists and workers of Plum Island," he relates, as well as directors of the Plum Island Animal Disease Center, who provided "initial cooperation." He pored through a huge number of U.S. government documents, many in the National Archives in Washington, D.C. He also made heavy use of the U.S. Freedom of Information Act.

A key Carroll finding: a "founding father" of the U.S. government's biological warfare operation on Plum Island was Dr. Erich Traub, and Traub, during World War II, had been "lab chief of Insel Riems—a secret biological warfare laboratory" operated on an island in the Baltic Sea by Germany's Nazi government.[80] "Traub worked directly for Adolph Hitler's seond-in-charge, SS Reichsfurer Heinrich Himmler, on live germ trials," Carroll wrote in *Lab 257*. "He packaged weaponized foot-and-mouth disease virus, which was dispersed…onto cattle and reindeer" in the Soviet Union. And that, with the beginnings of the Cold War conflict between the Unied States and the Soviet Union, became the mission of the U.S. government facility on Plum Island—initially based in a laboratory with the name Lab 257—to do exactly what the documents McDonald of *Newsday* found was its Cold War mission: to kill Soviet livestock.

Lab 257 was originally a building used at Fort Terry for the storage of weapons, among these weapons were mines. It was converted to be used by the U.S. Army Chemical Corps for its biological warfare activities.

Traub came to the United States after World War II, wrote Carroll, under Operation Paperclip—the same United States government program that resulted in other Nazi scientists being brought to the United States, including Wernher von Braun. They were said to have only been "nominal participants in Nazi activies," wrote Carroll. "But the zealous [U.S.] military" recruited "many of whom had dark Nazi pasts." Traub had been in the United States before World War II and was engaged in Nazi activities then. In the 1930s, Traub was involved with Amerika-Deutscher Volksbund, which established Camp Siegfield in Yaphank, Long Island, "just 30 miles west of Plum Island," noted Carroll, as "the national headquarters of the American Nazi movement. Over forty thousand people throughout the New York region arrived by train, bus, and car to participate in Nuremberg-like rallies" at the camp. Meanwhile, "Traub spent the prewar period of his scientific career on a fellowship at the Rockefeller Institute in Princeton, New Jersey, perfecting his skills in viruses and bacteria under the tutelage of American experts before returning to Nazi Germany on the eve of the war."

Returning to the U.S. under Operation Paperclip after World War II and "just months into his Paperclip contract," Traub was invited by "the germ warriors of Fort Detrick, the army's biological warfare headquarters in Frederick, Maryland, and CIA operatives…for a talk," Carroll related. In *Lab 257*, he reveals a "declassified top-secret summary" of the meeting with Traub at Fort Detrick. "Dr. Traub," it says, "is a noted authority on viruses and diseases…This interrogation revealed much information of value to the animal disease program form a biological warfare point of view." Carroll wrote that "Traub's detailed explanation of the secret operation on Insel Riems and his activities there during the war…laid the groundwork for Detrick's offshore germ warfare animal disease lab on Plum Island." "Everybody seemed willing to forget about Erich Traub's dirty past," wrote Carroll. "They seemed willing to overlook that, in the

1930s, he faithfully attended Camp Siegfried." Traub was present at the dedication of the Plum Island facility.

Then, in 1954, the Plum Island focus changed. Carroll explains that "the importance" of the biological warfare work on Plum Island "was suddenly called into question" by the Pentagon. "The joint chiefs found that a war with the USSR would best be fought with conventional and nuclear means and biological warfare against humans—not against food animals. Destroying the food supply meant having to feed millions of starving Russians after winning a war."[81]

Did biological warfare work on Plum Island end in 1954? That's an open question. For example, in 1977, *Newsday* published an article by investigative reporters Drew Featherston and John Cummings about an outbreak of African Swine Fever in Cuba in 1971 that involved the CIA—and also, possibly, the Plum Island Animal Disease Center. The piece related how the outbreak of the disease resulted in the slaughter of 500,000 pigs, with pork a Cuban staple, to prevent further spread. It was the first and only time African swine fever, indigenous to East Africa, had struck the Western Hemisphere. The introduction of African swine fever, according to the *Newsday* piece, began with a container of the virus coming to a U.S. Army base, Fort Gulick, and CIA training ground in the then United States–run Canal Zone in Panama. The container was brought by boat to Cuba, put ashore near the U.S. Navy base at Guantanamo Bay and delivered to anti-Castro operatives. Two months later, the outbreak of African swine fever occurred. The only place where the virus was known to have been kept in the United States before the outbreak in Cuba was at the Plum Island Animal Disease Center. Then U.S. congressman Tom Downey of Amityville on Long Island expressed outrage. "It is preposterous that the U.S. government tried to destroy portions of the population's food," he declared.[82]

In 1971, Karl Grossman of *Newsday*'s daily newspaper competitor on Long Island, the *Long Island Press*, was investigating Plum Island and the biological warfare work done there. He was told by a spokesman for its then-manager, the U.S. Department of Agriculture, that biological warfare research of a "defensive" kind was done at the Plum Island Animal Disease Center. The research on Plum Island, the public relations man claimed, principally involved studying foreign animal diseases to prevent them from getting to livestock in the United States. This admission came on the eve of the first time journalists were allowed on Plum Island, on October 21, 1971. That day, Grossman's front-page story involving the spokesperson's acknowledgement of "defensive" biological warfare research was published.

Journalists—Grossman among them—many from national publications, were on the tour. "The laboratory's director, Dr. Jerry J. Callis," reported the *New York Times*, "said the tour was being held in response to numerous requests by newsmen over the years who wanted to see the little-known laboratory. It was clear that lab officials hoped the tour would dispel the 'biological warfare' rumors."[83]

Grossman wrote about the tour, again in a front-page *Long Island Press* article published the day after it as held. His piece included how, during the tour, in one laboratory area, a scientist in a white coat held up a tiny vial and explained to the journalists that its contents could infect ten thousand trillion cattle with foot-and-mouth disease. That, the scientist went on, was all the cattle that lived on the Earth—indeed, all the cattle "that ever" lived on the Earth. Why, Grossman asked, was so much foot-and-mouth disease virus needed? "We're not using it for biological warfare," the scientist exclaimed, "but to make vaccines."

Grossman visited the Plum Island Animal Disease Center twice in years afterward—including in 1978, when the foot-and-mouth disease virus escaped from the supposedly airtight Building 100 (constructed to replace Lab 257) and infected cattle in holding pens outside. The Department of Agriculture opened the center to local officials and journalists in the aftermath of this outbreak.

Grossman, in his syndicated column in many Long Island newspapers after the *Long Island Press* ceased publication, Carroll in *Lab 257* and John Loftus in an earlier book pursued a link between Plum Island and Lyme disease—first identified in Old Lyme, Connecticut, just across the Long Island Sound from Plum Island.

The Belarus Secret: The Nazi Connection in America, published in 1982 and written by Loftus, an attorney who had specialized in pursuing Nazis for the Office of Special Investigations of the U.S. Department of Justice, told of former "Nazi germ warfare scientists," brought to the United States after World War II, who "experimented with poison ticks dropped from planes to spread rare diseases. I have received some information suggesting that the U.S. tested some of these poison ticks on the Plum Island artillery range during the early 1950s....Most of the germ warfare records have been shredded, but there is a top-secret U.S. document confirming that 'clandestine attacks on crops and animals' took place at this time."[84] Loftus points to "the hypothesis that the poison ticks are the source of the Lyme disease spirochete." And he added: "Sooner or later, the whole truth will come out, but probably not in my lifetime."

Lab 257 notes that Lyme disease "surfaced" ten miles from Plum Island "in Old Lyme, Connecticut, in 1975," and it cites years of experimentation with ticks on Plum Island and the likelihood of an accidental or purposeful release. "The tick is the perfect germ vector," Carroll wrote in *Lab 257*, "which is why it has long been fancied as a germ weapon by early bio-warriors from Nazi Germany and the Empire of Japan to the Soviet Union and the United States." Carroll added, "A source who worked on Plum Island in the 1950s recalls that animal handlers and a scientist released ticks outdoors on the island. 'They called him the Nazi scientist.'"

After the 9/11 attack, Plum Island's management was shifted from the Department of Agriculture to the Department of Homeland Security. The U.S. government had become highly concerned about an attack on Plum Island by terrorists. A 2003 report by the Government Accountability Office titled "Combatting Bioterrorism, Actions Needed to Improve Security at Plum Island Animal Disease Center" found that "fundamental concerns leave the facility vulnerable to security breaches."[85]

Grossman, in a 2005 column published by the *New York Times*, headed "Target: Plum Island," wrote how "Plum Island has a major and unfixable problem: it's an easy target for terrorists, indeed a sitting duck." The Plum Island Animal Disease Center, "in the wake of 9/11, the center, housing highly virulent disease agents a mile and a half off Long Island, constitutes a serious risk not just to New York, but also to Connecticut, Massachusetts and Rhode Island, which are all within 100 miles of Plum Island." The Grossman column cited the 2003 Government Accountability Office report and noted how it found that there a substantial risk that "an adversary might try to steal pathogens" from Plum Island to use them against people or animals in the United States. "The report noted that there were pathogens on Plum Island lethal to both animals and humans. A camel pox strain being researched at the center, it warned, could be converted into "an agent as threatening as smallpox," and the Venezuelan equine encephalitis virus being studied could be "developed into a human biowarfare agent." Also, the report emphasized that the center "was not designed to be a highly secure facility."

"This is not idle anxiety," the column went on. Cited was the story of a 2002 raid of the Kabul, Afghanistan residence of Sultan Bashiruddin Mahmood, a nuclear physicist who American officials had identified as an associate of Osama bin Laden. CIA operatives and army commandos found a "dossier" containing "information on a place in New York called the Plum Island Animal Disease Center."

And it's easy to see why terrorists would find Plum Island an easy target. The main laboratory (Building 100) sits along the island's northern coast. Indeed, the ferries that shuttle passengers between Orient Point and New London, Conn., pass directly in front of the building. From a boat, terrorists armed with shoulder-fired rockets would have a clear shot. Diving a plane into the main lab would be simple. Moreover, terrorists who managed to get on the island would find little resistance. The General Accounting Office report found serious security flaws.

The column concluded that Plum Island "is just too dangerous....Work involving highly toxic pathogens that requires the highest bio-safety level should be done at a heavily guarded facility inland, perhaps constructed underground."[86]

Planned as a replacement of the Plum Island Animal Disease Center, the U.S. government is now constructing—at a cost of $1.25 billion—a National Bio and Agro-Defense Facillity in Kansas, despite protests from Kansans that the facility would be in the middle of "cattle country" in the United States. It is slated become operational in 2022 or 2023.

The federal government, in recent years, has called for the sale of Plum Island; indeed, Donald Trump, before being elected U.S. president, sought to buy Plum Island and build a golf course on it. "It would be a really beautiful, world-class golf course," Trump said in *Newsday* interview. But following political pressure by some Long Island environmentalists and politicians, the sale of Plum Island has been blocked, and the scheme, as of this writing is to preserve the island and also let research continue on it. Carroll says this is folly. "The island is an environmental disaster," says Carroll. "You can't let anybody on it....There is contamination all over the island," and thus, it needs to be "forsaken." Until recent decades, all the waste generated on Plum Island stayed there—some incinerated but some buried in numerous locations. As for government jobs, Carroll says, "It is utter foolishness to try to save 200 jobs at the price of protecting the entire region from this island and the threat it represents." An outbreak of disease agents worked with on Plum Island—notably those affecting both animals and people—in the heavily populated area off which the island sits could be "devastating."[87]

6

RUSSIAN SPIES IN THE SHADOWS OF SUBURBIA

In the decade following the end of World War II, Long Island became home to dozens of Nike and BOMARC (Boeing Michigan Aeronautical Research Center) nuclear warhead missile sites and a booming innovation hub for Cold War military technology. With the creation of Brookhaven National Laboratory and establishment of a government laboratory on Plum Island, the United States was in competition with the Soviet Union to staff these facilities with the most qualified and innovative scientific minds, even if it was equivalent to making deals with war criminals. At the end of the World War II, Nazi scientists were looking to leave Germany and escape prosecution for war crimes. With pressure from former vice president Henry Wallace, who argued that these war criminal scientists could develop competitive military and civilian industries, hiring them became priority.[88] To further organize these efforts, the CIA created the Office of Scientific Intelligence. In August 1949, the CIA met to discuss the nominations to critical lists of scientists who had been on a denial-of-entry list into Austria. Many of these scientists were in the Soviet-occupied part of Germany. Priority scientists were involved in the fields of atomic energy, biological warfare, chemical warfare, electronics in warfare, guided missiles, aircraft, undersea warfare and medicine.[89] These scientists would remain under military jurisdiction after they were hired and until it is shown that they had done satisfactory work. They would be permitted to take the steps to legalize their stay in the United States.[90] This program and the emerging nuclear arms race heightened the use of secret intelligence operations in the Soviet Union and United States. Laboratories such Kelly Wilbur E. Associated Nucleonics of Garden City, which was active in the Joint Committee on Atomic Energy, were under CIA surveillance daily. Top engineers in Republic, Grumman and Brookhaven Laboratory had FBI clearances updated daily. Even with all the monitoring and precautions taken by federal officials, Soviets would find gaps in security.

Soviet presence in Long Island would come not only in the form of a Russian neighbor but in the form of a Soviet government. In October 1946, the sleepy North Shore city of Glen Cove was turned upside down. The old secluded Killenworth Estate had been the home of the late George Dupont Pratt. The estate was originally located on five thousand acres and featured a thirty-nine-room mansion with guest houses in a Tudor Revival architectural style. By the late 1940s, the main mansion and remaining thirty-six acres were assessed to be worth $500,000, but they were sold for an estimated $1 million. The purchaser was Vyacheslav Molotov, Joseph Stalin's right-hand man. Molotov, the appointed foreign minister for the Soviet Union, became prominent at the United Nations in Lake Success. Once the sale went public, the city attempted to displace the new owners.

The first fight was over a tax lien, for which Molotov argued he was over-assessed. The Soviets paid a total of $7,324 in taxes, justifying that it was the true assessed value. The $7,324 payment was paid in 1950, but no full payments were made until 1961, when the estate filed for a tax exemption. Congressman Steve Derounian of Roslyn appealed to the Kennedy administration to reimburse Glen Cove the $25,000 a year in back taxes, and if extended as an exemption, an additional $10,000 for other fees and fines the estate accumulated.[91] The public fight over the Glen Cove City tax would be waged until 1966, when the estate was granted tax-exempt status due to it being used as the primary residence of the Soviet ambassador and the grounds being used as a recreational facility for other diplomats. Like the German consulate reaching out to German Bund members for recruitment as spies during World War II, Molotov's presence in Long Island stirred fears of a similar threat. These fears of Soviet spies were further flamed with the arrest of Ethel and Julius Rosenberg. Ethel and Julius were accused of copying hundreds of government documents that had been stolen from a Columbia University safe.[92] Most notably, the pair were accused of being involved in the passing of nuclear secrets to the Soviets. The nuclear intelligence was believed to have been stolen by Ethel's younger brother, David Greenglass, who worked at Los Alamos Laboratory. But once they received Greenglass's intelligence, the Soviets deemed it useless.[93] When

The Glen Cove Killenworth Estate, which was purchased by Soviet foreign minister Vyacheslav Molotov in the late 1940s. *Courtesy of the Library of Congress, Image Collection.*

caught, David was pressured to give testimony against his sister and brother-in-law to avoid prosecution. The testimony and details of the case exposed the alleged Rosenberg's drop-off point for the thirty-five-millimeter film was on the platform of Glen Cove Train Station. With the proximity to the Soviet compound, many felt it was more than a coincidence to have Glen Cove as a drop-off destination.

In 1952, the North Shore community of Upper Brookville was caught off guard when the Soviet chief delegate to the United States Valerian Zorin purchased the historic Norwich House. The Norwich House, later named Miller Estate, was comprised of fourteen acres and a nineteen-thousand-square-foot mansion. The purchase price from the Soviet government was undisclosed. The public anxiety around the new neighbors in Glen Cove and Brookville attracted the attention of the CIA. The CIA started surveilling to compile a list of people who were coming and going from both estates. The mayor of Glen Cove and all the mayors up to 1982 wrote letters to the CIA requesting full disclosure of any illegal activities at the estate. The letters would go on to explain that Glen Cove was losing thousands of dollars in tax revenue with the tax exemption for an estate that only served as a spy center.[94] Glen Cove's new Russian neighbors were not quiet and cost the city and the county thousands of dollars daily for security. This overhead cost was about to reach its peak in late September and early October 1960, when the world descended on Glen Cove.

On September 23, 1960, the State Department contacted Nassau County and the City of Glen Cove to inform them that Soviet Premier Nikita Khrushchev was visiting the Killenworth Estate. This would be Khrushchev's second visit to the United States. Nassau police commissioner Andrew Kirk and Glen Cove's police chief Charles Reinfeld started to assemble a security force around the compound and detail a safeguard route for Khrushchev's motorcade. In total, 125 Nassau County police, working in shifts of thirty-five men, armed with tear gas, machine guns, shotguns and a team of bloodhounds, were deployed.[95] All roads and highways would be closed for the motorcade, and the federal government demanded no restrictions for Khrushchev around the city of Glen Cove. Additional support came from State Department agents patrolling the surrounding airspace by helicopters. An undisclosed number of helicopters would have snipers in place to prevent any assassination threat. The Khrushchev visit was to be the largest security operation in Long Island history—and for good reason. While planning the local security, residents were emotionally charged and expressed their outrage in having Khrushchev come to Glen Cove. Prior to the announcement of Khrushchev's arrival, tensions were almost at a tipping point with the arms race and emerging space race. In October 1957, the Soviets launched the first satellite, *Sputnik*; in 1958, the Soviets shot down a transport plane, arguing it was in Soviet airspace; and in May 1960, the Soviets shot down an American U-2 spy plane in their airspace and captured pilot Francis Gary Powers. While the visit was being planned, the Soviet Union was holding Powers, and the KGB forced him to apologize publicly for spying, which became a public embarrassment for the United States. These events led the local American Legionnaires to hang a Khrushchev effigy and burn it in spots they thought the motorcade would pass through. Olga Wrangel, a seventy-eight-year-old resident of Sea Cliff, publicly told fellow residents that she wanted to plant a bomb at the estate or on the motorcade route.[96] Mayor Joseph Suozzi, in a statement to *Newsday*, said the city would be doing "business as usual....We'll just ignore him." The Lion's Club agreed with the plan and decorated all possible motorcade routes with U.S. flags. On September 24, Khrushchev's schedule was set, and he was expected to arrive on Saturday, October 1, at 12:05 p.m. sharp. His entourage included representatives from Soviet satellite countries, and at

5:12 p.m., United Arab Republic president Gamal Nasser would arrive for a closed-door meeting. Some twenty reporters would interview Nasser and Khrushchev at 6:28 p.m. from the estate's driveway. On Sunday, at 11:25 a.m., Wladyslaw Gomulka, the Polish communist leader, would join Khrushchev at the estate for afternoon meetings, and at 4:30 p.m., Khrushchev would meet with Ghana's president Kwame Nkrumah for another closed-door meeting. Then, on Sunday, at 6:05 p.m., the security forces would be assembled for Khrushchev's departure back to New York City.

Mayor Joseph Suozzi's request to have the locals ignore Khrushchev's visit fell on deaf ears. The following day, after the schedule was announced, Khrushchev arrived earlier than expected to throw off any potential threats. More than five thousand anticommunist demonstrators turned up, holding signs that read "Fat Pig Murderer" and "Chubby Russian Hangman" while booing at the motorcade as it passed through the estate's gates.[97] Later in the day, the Latvian American Organization and Federation of Former Hungarian Political Prisoners, led by Dr. Bela Fabian, head of the Former Hungarian Political Prisoners Federation, handed out black-striped robes, replicas of Soviet prison uniforms, and organized demonstrators to chant, "Khrush the fat red rat."[98] While driving through Glen Cove, protesters threw eggs at Khrushchev's limousine, forcing it to turn back to New York City to reassess security. After double-checking the protocol of the state department and local law enforcement, the motorcade proceeded to Glen Cove and arrived to thousands of protestors. Khrushchev's unexpected visit and the unpredictable number of protesters dwarfed the surprise of locals when they found out his stay was closer to two weeks than the originally planned weekend. While the city of Glen Cove broke down into daily protests, with an army of reporters representing global media outlets, the compound was hosting critical diplomatic meetings that were shaping Soviet relations with North Africa and Latin America. On the same day that Khrushchev came to Glen Cove, he was at the UN, watching Fidel Castro build up an alliance that exported the communist revolution to the Arab and North African world. Castro held a series of closed-door meetings with Gamal Nasser in Harlem's Hotel Theresa, and later, during UN sessions, Castro, Nasser, Saeb Salaam of Lebanon and Marshal Tito of Yugoslavia were in dialogue. Castro, an ally of the Soviet Union, when confronted about the meeting, explained he was working on a dialogue in an effort to build a block of neutral nations in the UN.

With the UN activity, reporters would consult Khrushchev for updates on his daily driveway press conferences. But the only questions he gave concise

Nikita Khrushchev at the United Nations in 1960. While attending the 1960 general assembly session, he was staying at Killenworth Estate in Glen Cove. *Courtesy of the Library of Congress, Image Collection.*

responses to were about the Soviet space program. In the press conference, he reported, "Everything is ready for a Soviet attempt to put a man into space, and I sympathize with America's failed attempts."[99] In the following days at the Glen Cove compound, Gamal Nasser and Ghana's president Kwame Nkrumah met with Khrushchev and other Soviet satellite leaders in a series of meetings. On October 2, Khrushchev arranged a meeting with the Algerian Nationalists Provisional Government at Glen Cove. Prior to this meeting, Algeria was trying to seek recognition from the UN as a legitimate government to affirm its independence from France. Its war for independence had been fought since 1954, but it had not received Soviet recognition due to the rebels falling short in declaring themselves communist. But like Ghana, Cuba and Lebanon, which were all in talks relating to Algeria, Algeria embraced the fundamental communist principal of decolonization and wanted the Soviets to extend recognition. The Soviet Union publicly expressed its support for global decolonization but had remained silent up to this point on Algeria. In total, eighteen nations recognized Algeria's Liberation Front government, but it lacked support from any of the main global powers. Belkacem Krim, vice-premier of the Algerian provisional government, and Minister of Finance Ahmed Francis met with the Soviets in their first official meeting, in which they would directly ask for support through recognition.[100] The following day, Khrushchev announced to the press in the driveway, "Algerian rebels should keep up the fight against France, and I am in full agreement with the liberation of Algeria."[101] On October 10, the State Department instructed Glen Cove officials that Khrushchev would leave on Thursday, October 13, for the Idlewild Airport (present-day day John F. Kennedy Airport). Before leaving, Khrushchev told reporters that he commended the professionalism of the county and city police and joked that he might stay for another two weeks.

The compounds would not only serve as a global political backdrop but also become suspected of generating a Soviet spy ring that may have been embedded within the Long Island communities. As the Glen Cove and Brookville compounds sheltered Soviet diplomats, a series of skilled spies and handlers attempted to weave themselves into the fabric of the Long Island communities. These spies masked themselves as middle-class, average neighbors, but some publicly stood out as least likely to be associated with Soviets or communists.

Robert Glenn Thompson of 1693 North Gardiner Lane, Bay Shore, originally from Detroit, was the owner of the local company Best Fuel Oil Service. Thompson boasted that he had over nine hundred customers and had to lease an old gas station on 345 Little East Neck Road in Babylon to grow his booming business. His wife was German-born, and they had three children who came off as God-fearing, wearing their religion on their sleeves in discussions. He was an unapologetic Barry Goldwater supporter and was vocal in his hatred for communists. He bragged about his service in the air corps during World War II, but many believed he exaggerated his combat history, due to him being only twenty-nine years old in 1963, which would have made him ten years old in 1945. His stories of his military service varied from being an airplane mechanic to working with the secret service in Berlin or training military dogs. Most neighbors mainly described him as a not-too-smart, chain smoking bigot. Benjamin Young, a Black man who lived next to Thompson, and his family were terrorized by Thompson's racist actions. Thompson, angered that a Black family had purchased the house next door to him, put up signs in his front yard that said, "For Sale— Mixed Neighbors."[102] Following the sign incident, Thompson hung a noose facing the Young house and used racial slurs when he saw Young and his family. Thompson's employees referred to him as having dramatic mood swings and living off pills due to a recent heart attack. On Gardiner Lane, his house stood out not for its simple white-shingled siding or red front door but for the large fifty-foot-tall shortwave radio antenna that towered over it. The Young family used to complain to friends that noises could be heard coming from the Thompsons' basement, such as hammering or banging at 3:00 and 4:00 a.m. But the Youngs would underplay the noise, saying it was just Thompson being a spiteful neighbor.

On January 7, 1965, as Thompson sat in his office on Little East Neck Road in Babylon, FBI agents surrounded the property, stormed in his office and arrested him in front of his employees. Later in the day, a dozen agents surrounded his North Gardiner Lane home and conducted a detailed search of the property while all his neighbors looked on in surprise. As soon as he was taken into custody, he retained the services of local lawyer Sidney Siben from the law firm of Siben and Siben. He was taken to the U.S. District Court in Brooklyn and charged with espionage and supplying intelligence information to the Soviet Union relating to military installations, missile sites, code books and other activities related to the U.S. government in conspiracy with a Russian nationals.[103] Prior to the arraignment, Sidney Siben, after having discussions with the federal prosecutor and receiving the paperwork of the detailed accounts of his client's accused activities, posed many challenges for a defense. Thompson was one of four men in spy ring that was formed out of the Soviet embassy in Washington, D.C. The three other men included embassy counselor Boris V. Karpovich, also known as John Kurlinsky; another embassy official referred to as Steve; and Fedor Kudashkin, an interpreter at the United Nations in New York. When not in contact with the other three coconspirators, Thompson would report his progress directly to Moscow in the early hours of the morning under a series of code names and phrases with his shortwave radio station at his house. The designated meet-up locations for the conspirators included East Berlin; Thompson's childhood home in Detroit; Great Falls, Montana; the Lynbrook Train Station parking lot, specifically next to the Sailor and Soldiers Monument; Valley Stream Train Station; Oakdale Train Station; and various locations in Copiague. The identities of the Soviet agents were deduced based on different colored lighters used to light a cigarette at the station. At these locations, conversations were conducted inside a 1959 blue Chevrolet. During the Long Island meetings in the first five months of 1962, Russian agents would ask Thompson about the different personalities in Long Island and his neighbors' beliefs.[104] These observations of locals were how Thompson shaped his own cover identity. At one of these daily meetings in Lynbrook, a laundry truck was taking notes and monitoring them. But this was not the first time federal agents watched Thompson. Since he was in the air force back in 1957, the federal government was able to trace back to when he was first hired by Soviets. The indictment then traced back to Thompson receiving $300 for disclosing details about the Rouge Park missile site near Detroit to Soviet agent Hemet Kurlinsky.[105] In further testimony from his brother Stephen Thompson, "a Russian named Steven came to his childhood Detroit home back in 1959 and asked why did Thompson not contact him and please contact him."[106] Most surprising of all was that Thompson had been questioned by local authorities for his suspicious actions prior to his arrest, and Thompson told Siben he fully cooperated. In response to the indictment, Thompson pleaded innocent and was released on $15,000 bail.

The following day, every media outlet ran stories about not only Thompson's indictment but also his personal encounters, which included tall tales of military service while at local barbecues, conflicts with his Black neighbors, his support for Goldwater and his claims of a growing business. In an interview with the *New York Times*, Thompson stated he was "100% American, and all these accusations are not true." He further explained that he was concerned about his nine hundred customers leaving him and that he had nothing against Black people, the dispute with the Young family was "related to his and their kids not getting along," but he said nothing else relating to the indictment.[107] In a separate interview with *Long Island Press* reporter Karl Grossman, Thompson said he was the target of federal agents because the air force wanted him to reenlist and he refused to cooperate. Following the arraignment, the State Department expelled Boris Vladimiro Karpovich, making his departure the second highest-ranked Soviet official to ever be ordered out of America. In the initial sentencing, the prosecutors were pushing for the death penalty. After a month to think about it, with his attorney evaluating the prosecutor's strong case, the only hope was to work out a plea deal to avoid a death sentence. Thompson changed his not guilty plea to one of guilty on March 9, 1965. Thompson detailed that he was guilty of working with Soviet espionage agents for a total of six years, from June 1957 to July 1963. He defected to work with the Soviets not for their communist ideals but because he was disgruntled about a court-martial for public drunkenness, which led to his dishonorable discharge. During this time, Thompson was given $1,000 from Soviet agents to build his shortwave radio station, and he gave them, on average, fifty to one hundred documents and photographs every two weeks.[108] While pleading guilty, he further detailed that he was recruited in West Berlin, where he received training by East German and Soviet officials. While living on Long Island, Thompson provided the Soviets with information about the island's water reservoirs, gas line locations, local power plants locations and gas tank storage information.[109] Thompson, in a statement, further apologized to the court and stated the guilty plea was for his children and an attempt to avoid a lengthy trial. Thompson then went on to explain, "It was tearing me up. What I was doing, it was tearing me up, and I didn't care if I was caught. After a while, I was afraid of fear itself and contemplated suicide. I am glad it is finally over with."[110] Following his plea, his sentencing hearing was set for early May, and he was allowed to remain on bail. Once an outgoing, social person among his neighbors, Thompson remained self-isolated within the walls of his Gardiner Lane home until his sentencing date.

Soviet spy and Bay Shore resident Robert Thompson in court in 1965. *Courtesy of the New York State Courts.*

In early May, at Robert Thompson's sentencing, his lawyer reminded the court of his client's cooperation and asked for lenience in his sentence. The judge sentenced Thompson to thirty years in prison with the possibility of parole after twenty years. In a statement following the sentencing, the judge, Walter Bruchhausen, stated:

> *This court is confronted with one of the most difficult decisions facing any court. The defendant was engaged during a period of six years, here and abroad, in undermining our national security. The consequence thereof is readily determinable. It is clear that your criminal activities warrant this severe punishment.*[111]

Once sentenced, Thompson was taken into custody to begin serving his time at the federal prison in Lewisburg, Pennsylvania. Thompson remained in federal prison until April 1978. In the spring of 1978, tensions were elevated, with an increasing number of Soviet and U.S.—or allied—agents being taken as prisoners abroad in Chile, Israel and Mozambique. One prisoner, Myron Marcus, was an Israeli who was being held in Soviet-allied

Mozambique. Marcus, a businessman who frequently had business dealings in South Africa, had his plane make an emergency landing in Mozambique, where he was taken prisoner. Congressman Benjamin Gilman represented Rockland County, New York, which was a politicly active Orthodox Jewish district. Within this community, the cause was taken up to free Marcus. With pressure from Congressman Gilman, a prisoner exchange agreement was made between the Soviets and America. Robert Thompson was released from federal prison and deported to East Germany, and Marcus was released from Mozambique and sent to Israel.

Soviet spy operations were not only confined to the recruitment of former or current members of the military. Long Island was a hub for military innovation, and defense plants such as Grumman were on the cutting edge for developing fighter planes. In 1972, the F-14 Tomcat was introduced and became one of the iconic Cold War–era fighter planes. The Soviets wanted to replicate its engineering and find the weaknesses of the plane in combat. Both the Soviet Union and the United States were in a race for engineers, and the Soviets were trying to lure as many military engineers as possible to become industry spies. Valery Markelov, a Soviet translator employed by the United Nations during the day, was a recruiter for industry spies in the evening. Markelov, a fixture at many engineering conferences, attended these meetings and observed the various personalities of the attendees. Having a background in engineering himself and teaching various courses in engineering, Markelov had a strong understanding and passion for the trade. In 1969, Grumman was working on a new fighter plane with groundbreaking technology that included wings that could change angles in flight and a two-hundred-mile-wide radar capability. This groundbreaking fighter plane would be known as the F-14 Tomcat, and it was a game changer for combat operations.

At a tradeshow in a Hicksville hotel and convention center, Markelov met recently hired Bethpage Grumman engineer Bill Van Zwienen of Bay Shore. Zwienen, at the time, was going through a bitter divorce and staying in a Bellmore boardinghouse. This was a perfect time to sway him to make extra money on the side, even if it would mean being an industry spy. But Zwienen was not as vulnerable as Markelov expected. When approached at the tradeshow, Markelov exchanged information with Zwienen and expressed his wiliness to learn more about the new F-14 prototypes. With fears of industry secrets being leaked, all defense plants formed a security force to keep the engineering data, prototypes and drafts of blueprints under lock and key. The engineers to the military contracts were closely and, in some cases, secretly monitored. Harry Volz, Grumman's director of security, was in charge of the activities at the Bethpage Plant, and Zwienen became well acquainted with him. Concerned about his conversation with Markelvo and thinking he might be a spy, Zwienen went to Volz. Volz, in response, notified the FBI, who contacted Zwienen for help in apprehending Markelvo. Zwienen set up a series of meetings and fed known or false information to Markelvo for seventeen months. During these meetings, Markelvo supplied film for a thirty-five-millimeter camera and set up a secret code for greeting each other. At the close of each meeting, Zwienen was paid between $50 and $400.

Markelvo's meetings were held in different locations across the South Shore, but they mostly took place at local restaurants. The meetings were held at the former Seascape Restaurant in Islip (now JR Steak house on Montauk Highway), various restaurants in Amityville and Pietro's in Freeport. While at these meetings, Markelvo would critique the food in an effort to make small talk, but he mainly ordered steak. By early 1972, the FBI had caught four Soviet spies with cover jobs in the UN and subverting various industries throughout America. These arrests came on the heels of rising tensions and President Nixon's upcoming trip to Moscow. As Zwienen parked his car at the Wah Chinese Restaurant in Patchogue on February 14, he flicked his lights, signaling the FBI that Markelvo was present.[112] The FBI took Markelvo into custody, and he was arraigned in Brooklyn Federal Court. He was held on $500,000 bail, but the following day, his bail was lowered to $100,000, which was posted. By August, the charges were overturned, and Markelvo returned to the Soviet Union. The court's decision came on the eve of President Nixon's trip to Moscow, which was seen as an effort to create an amicable atmosphere between the two countries.[113] The 1972 Markelvo case was not the last of the Soviets' attempts to obtain military secrets on Long Island.

In the mid-1970s and early 1980s, Cold War tensions were starting to thaw. Nixon's Moscow visit led to the Strategic Arms Limitation Talks (SALT). These talks resulted in a series a treaties that paved the way in slowing militarization between the Soviets and America. The centerpiece of Nixon's talks was the Anti-Ballistic Missile Treaty, which set limitations on ballistic missiles that are used in delivering a nuclear warhead. This cooling of tensions was a breakthrough, but it was a false sense of security to believe that the Soviet spy threat was in the past.

In Glen Cove, the Cold War was heating up at the Soviet compound. By 1970, the Soviet compound had a tax/city debt of $49,000, which the city was attempting to collect, but the compound's biggest threat was the Jewish Defense League. During the Israeli Six Day War, the Soviet Union was aligned itself with the United Arab Republic under Gamal Nasser, which led to a total breakdown of Soviet and Israeli diplomatic ties. Within the Soviet Union, there was deep antisemitism, and many Soviet Jewish people were unable to leave due to the Jewish Refusenik policy, which banned Jewish people from leaving the country. Within the Jewish enclaves of New York City and parts of Long Island, the Jewish Defense League (JDL) rallied against the rising Soviets and local antisemitism. Local members of the JDL and the Jewish community started to view the Glen Cove compound as a symbol of hate. On January 3, 1971, five hundred JDL members marched from Roosevelt Flied to Glen Cove. Dozens of the demonstrators were dressed in prison outfits with Stars of David; another group of demonstrators was following the marchers in a motorcade of an estimated seven hundred cars. At the head of the motorcade was a flatbed truck with a makeshift jail cell and people dressed as prisoners inside. Once they reached the compound, they released a sea of red balloons that read "Let My People Go."[114] The march made page 1 in local news, but more drastic techniques were employed. The largest economic protest was the JDL's attempt to buy the $49,000 tax lien from the city against the Soviet compound. These efforts were led by Glen Cove resident and JDL national chairman Rabbi Meir Kahane. Dressed in army fatigues and berets, the JDL marched into Glen Cove City Hall and attempted to buy the debt in an effort to evict the Soviets; they said they would make the estate a museum for Soviet atrocities and a headquarters for a Soviet government in exile.[115] The city's mayor Andrew DiPaola had every intention of selling the debt to the JDL or anyone else who had the cash in hand, but a day prior to the JDL coming into city hall, the State Department contacted him and explained that he was in violation of federal law by not prohibiting interference with a foreign diplomat. He was warned that this sale could be punishable by three years in prison. In an interview with *Newsday*, DiPaola stated, "They [the State Department lawyers] told me that this thing had gone far enough and I had made my point."[116] When these legal efforts failed, the Soviet compound was vandalized with slogans on the driveway pillars that read "Let Our People Go"; there were also Stars of David and JDL letters. When confronted about the vandalism, the spokesman for the Soviet compound stated they had no intentions of pressing charges. These acts of protest only increased in the coming year. On June 22, 1971, JDL members Sheldon Seigel and Jacob Weisel of Brooklyn drove to the Soviet estate with fifteen sticks of dynamite and two blasting caps connected to a timing device, and they planted them next to the wall and shrubs of the estate's driveway gate. Following an anonymous tip, Glen Cove police were dispatched and found the bomb ten minutes before it was supposed to detonate. This bombing attempt outraged Soviet officials. The Soviet ambassador to the United States Yakov Malik demanded more safety measures and said that authorities needed to "take all measures to find the criminals who committed this criminal act."[117] By September, Seigel and Weisel had been captured and connected to the Amtorg (Soviet Union commercial agency) bombing in midtown Manhattan. Following these threats, many decided to turn down the combative politics against the compound. DiPaola, in an attempt to obtain more protection, wrote to President Richard Nixon, highlighting the daily demonstrations of sometimes seven thousand people at the compound's gates. The letter explained that Glen Cove was stretched thin with resources and needed more resources to hire more staff. The total amount requested from the United States was $100,000 a year. But the Soviets were using this as a diversion to organize more efforts in gathering military industrial secrets from the local defense plants.

In the summer of 1982, the Glen Cove Soviet compound had become extra quiet, and from the years prior, tensions seemed to level out between the city and the compound. Due to the protests turning violent in the years prior, KGB agents were stationed in the house. These agents were, at first, seen as extra security. Following the deployment of the initial nine KGB agents, large wooden boxes were seen being delivered, and what looked like a survey of the property was being conducted. The significance of the property's location was that it happened to be five miles from one American Telephone and Telegraph tower and twelve miles from another. The estate, coincidentally, was in the cross section of almost all phone communication lines on Long Island. A leak within the compound tipped off United States intelligence officers that the third floor of the compound contained the world's most advanced electric surveillance equipment. This claim was later confirmed by Arkady Shevchenko, a Soviet UN official who defected to United States. This equipment was used to tap into any phone call made to or from a defense plant and had special focus on certain defense engineers. One company that had electronic eavesdropping was Eaton Corporation's ALL Division in Deer Park, which specialized in electronic components for the B-1 Bomber. Dick Dunne, a spokesperson of the firm, assured that "little is ever said over the phone" and further explained, "All of our people are constantly kept aware of that type of thing because, by definition, what we do here is certainly important to the Soviets."[118] It was believed that this electronic spying was being conducted for at least four years and that uncountable amounts of information was recorded and sent back to the Kremlin. The second Soviet compound in Upper Brookville was confirmed to not be involved, and only the Glen Cove Estate was singled out for these operations. Once exposed to the public, tensions between the city and the compound were reignited.

Elected Mayor Alan Parente was outraged by the government's lack of action against the Soviets. In a *Newsday* interview, when asked how he dealt with the spy operations in the estate, Parente told reporters, "I think that while the federal government does have jurisdiction over foreign relationships, they don't have jurisdiction over who can use recreational facilities."[119] Following the interview, Glen Cove announced it would ban the Soviet compound residents from all city municipal golf courses and tennis courts. Following the ban, warm weather was forecasted, which would have been perfect beach weather. That August, Glen Cove's mayor and officials extended the municipal ban to all beaches and said that it applied to all Soviet compound workers. In late 1982, the Soviets reached out to the U.S. State Department for help. The State Department filed a court order to open the city's municipal services back up to the Soviet compound's residents and workers. Mayor Parente challenged the order, which gained him critics in other higher-ranking state officials and local congressman. New York City mayor Ed Koch called Glen Cove foolish and stated, "It would backfire on Glen Cove." While restricting the Soviets from Glen Cove amenities, Parente kept referring to the increased tax revenue needed to protect the compound. Local residents started to believe that the battle between the city and the Soviets was a distraction from local political events. Residents who were shopping in Glen Cove told *Newsday* reporters, "We are starting an international conflict here over a minor thing," and, "This seems to be a distraction to take people's mind off the tax increase the city is trying to push through."[120] Glen Cove would eventually drop the ban on the Soviets, and tensions leveled out under the newly elected mayor Vincent Suozzi in early 1984. Once elected, Suozzi gave resident stickers to all forty compound residents and successfully negotiated with the state department and local congressional lawmakers on getting a reimbursement for the city for the extra compound security.

It would take another thirty-two years and the fall of the Soviet Union to bring about another investigation into espionage. This investigation was against the Brookville compound, which was a headquarters for spy operations. The federal government locked down the compound the day after President Obama ordered it closed due to Russia's interference in the 2016 presidential election.[121] These headlines echoed the decades-old spying techniques and community tensions throughout the corridors of the Killenworth compound. In an interview following the closing of Brookville, Glen Cove mayor Reginald Spinello stated, "What happens behind its closed doors is anyone's guess."[122]

7

BUILDUP OF MILITARY AND NUCLEAR MISSILE BASES ON LONG ISLAND

During the Spanish-American War, military bases were built up around Long Island in an effort to make the waterways secure from potential invading forces. During World War II, an air base in Westhampton and Camp Hero in Montauk further connected a chain of Coast Guard and military facilities or gun emplacements to secure the island's entire shoreline. Mitchel Field in Uniondale provided air patrols throughout Nassau, Queens and Kings Counties and patrolled for submarines off the coast. With the end of World War II, many of the Coast Guard and military bases were either closed or merged, but with the heighted Soviet tensions, these bases got a new lease on life. Camp Hero, constructed with seventeen-inch-long antiaircraft guns built into bunkers and hundreds of feet of underground tunnels, was disguised as a fishing village to confuse potential enemy planes. Toward the end of the war, the base would become home to one of the military's most advanced radar systems. In 1948, the air force took over the Camp Hero Base and became home to the 773rd Radar Squadron. While home to the 773rd, Camp Hero would build a AN/FPS-35 long-range eighty-five-foot-tall radar tower. Able to detect objects from over two hundred miles away, the tower was one of the largest radar structures built in Untied States. The secrecy of the base and the daily reminder of the powerful antiaircraft guns being tested paved the way for urban myths and fictional stories of human experiments. The urban myths would become the base's best defense from locals or vacationers trying to trespass on the property to explore. But other military installations across the island were not as secretive and were even liabilities to surrounding communities.

This page: Camp Hero Montauk was home to the 773rd Radar Squadron. Pictured is the base and the squadron in 1958. *Courtesy of the Montauk Public Library.*

Mitchel Field, Uniondale, 1948. *Courtesy of the Cradle of Aviation.*

The activity of Nassau County's last remaining airbase within its growing suburban backdrop became a concern by the mid-1950s. After World War II, the Hempstead Plains area, home to potato fields prior to the war, then held over seventeen thousand homes built for returning veterans. On September 13, 1955, a B-25 bomber that was on its way back to Mitchel Field crashed in Uniondale, near a cemetery, killing the six crew members. This event drew concerns that the crash could have happened on a residential block. But while the base debated different flight patterns, the following month, a B-26 bomber crashed in East Meadow on the densely populated block of Barbara Drive. The crash happened during daylight hours, destroying the home of Paul Koroluck, who initially thought his family was killed as he watched the fire engulf his home. Koroluck would later find his family safe, but a total of two crew members were killed. Public pressure turned against the base, and local elected officials took up a platform to move the base due to safety reasons. While the calls to move the base became louder, the air force was facing a sizable budget cut of an estimated $100 million, which made the closure an achievable reality.[123] Between 1949 and 1958, there were fifteen recorded plane crashes either around the base or en

Major Charles Dryden by a T-33 jet trainer at Mitchel Air Force Base, 1956. *Courtesy of Hofstra University's Special Collections.*

route to the base, with a total of fifteen deaths. In combination with public pressure over safety and budget cuts, the air force's undersecretary Malcolm MacIntyre announced that Mitchel Field "very likely will be closed down within a year."[124] The air force cited that the closure of Mitchel Field's 1,168-acre base would have a net savings of $8 million a year. By 1961, the base was officially decommissioned.

The remaining sub-base to Mitchel Field was Suffolk County Air Force Base. Originally constructed during World War II, the base had a resurgence in 1951. The primary objective of the base was to defend the New York tristate area through its radar operations with Camp Hero in Montauk

On May 25, 1953, a B-25 crashed landed in East Meadow after engine failure. *Courtesy of the Cradle of Aviation.*

On October 1955, a B-26 bomber crashed in East Meadow. Pictured are the remains of the plane in the front yard of Paul Koroluck. *Courtesy of the Cradle of Aviation.*

and flight/missile interception systems. In mid-1963, the base became the primary station for the Fifty-Second Fighter Wing, which flew the F-86 Sabre and later the F-101 Voodoos supersonic jet. Flying these jets, the Fifty-Second mainly conducted submarine patrols off the coast of the island. In the decades that followed, locals would push to rename the Suffolk County Base to honor one of its bravest during World War II, Francis "Gabby" Gabreski. Gabby became famous as a top flying Ace and had a personal record of gunning down twenty-eight Nazi fighter planes in his Farmingdale-made Republic P-47 Thunderbolt.

As the Cold War progressed, bases were set up on Long Island to use nuclear-tipped missiles in an effort to shoot down Soviet bombers flying near or over Long Island to potentially carry out a bombing of New York City. In 1953, there were 841 nuclear weapons in the American arsenal, and by January 1961, the United States had fielded 18,686 atomic arms.[125] The plan was to have the nuclear warheads on the army's Nike Hercules missiles and on the air force's BOMARC missiles to detonate amid formations of Soviet bombers. This was before ground-to-air missiles had the ability to perform a direct hit on an airplane. By detonating a nuclear-tipped missile amid a formation of Soviet bombers, the notion was that many of the bombers would be blasted out of the sky. However, radioactivity would rain down on one of the fastest-growing population centers in the United States. Long Island, unlike some areas in the United States, had the distinctive threat of not only being involved in a nuclear attack by the Soviets but in being affected by an effort to prevent the attack. The United States military started to survey properties on Long Island that comprised forty to fifty acres in an effort to build nuclear-tipped missile sites. Many locals were concerned about the placement in or near densely populated areas. When proposing a site near Glen Cove, the military invited Glen Cove mayor Joseph Suozzi and Brookville police commissioner Charles Capobianco to Fort Bliss in Texas to discuss why it was essential to have these sites constructed.[126] This method was partially successful and paved the way for Long Island to have seven bases that utilized Nike Hercules nuclear-tipped missiles or the BOMARC missiles. The sites that utilized the Nike missiles were located in Lido Beach, Brookville, Lloyd Harbor, Rocky Point, Amityville and Queens Fort Tilden. An additional base for launching BOMARC nuclear-tipped missiles was constructed in Westhampton. The BOMARC base in Westhampton fielded fifty-six nuclear-tipped missiles. Each had its own building. The roofs of the buildings would open like clam shells, and the missiles would rise and be launched from the structures.

The Nike had a top speed of over 2,700 miles per hour, with a flight ceiling of 100,000 feet, and it had a nuclear warhead on its nose. The nuclear warheads on the Nike Hercules and BOMARC missiles had massive explosive power. The nuclear warheads on the Nike Hercules came in three sizes—with the explosive power of either three, twenty or thirty kilotons of TNT. The warheads on the BOMARC missiles had the power of ten kilotons. The power of these missiles was comparable to the strength of the atomic bomb dropped on Hiroshima, which was equal to thirteen kilotons of TNT. The Long Island bases were described by *New York Times* journalist Joseph Berger as "one of those infamous buttons of the Cold War—the switch that could fire a nuclear missile at a Soviet bomber and possibly lead to an apocalypse—can be found in a rust-eaten trailer in the scrub pine and oak on this sandbar."[127] The amount of radioactive fallout that might have descended on Long Island would have depended on the winds and the location of the detonations. The detonations would have occurred not far from the island, which was the biggest concern for residents. The Nike Hercules had a range of 87 miles, and the BOMARC a range of 250 miles. Long Island was not alone in having such bases. Other Nike Hercules and BOMARC bases were set up during the Cold War all over metropolitan areas in the United States. Chicago was one of the most armed areas in the country and had Nike Hercules bases surrounding its entire suburban and urban area. Each base had eight officers and more than one hundred other military personnel divided to control the launching of the missiles. The sites were managed twenty-four hours a day in order to have the warheads in the air and detonated within ten minutes of a command.

The former six-missile Nike Hercules base in Rocky Point is now the site of a U.S. Army Reserve Center, but components of the missile base remain, including a variety of structures and the missile silos. The Nike Hercules missiles were positioned underground in the silos. The base was operational from 1957 to 1974. What was the eighteen-missile Nike Hercules base in Amityville is now also a U.S. Army Reserve Center. There are hardly any remnants from its time as a missile base. The base was operational also from 1957 to 1974 as well.

Amityville had one of the largest missile bases on Long Island; it housed not only Nike Hercules missiles but also Ajax missiles without nuclear-tipped warheads. This base sat next to the campus of buildings owned by the Sisters of Saint Dominic. "Before the Ajax missiles were installed, local Boy Scout troops were given rides on the elevators that hoisted the missiles above ground, and when the Ajax was brought to the community,

One of the six nuclear bases with a Nike missile pointed toward the sky in Fort Tilden Queens. *Courtesy of the New York City Library, Digital Image Collections.*

the missiles were displayed in community July Fourth parades."[128] When the Nike Hercules missiles arrived, the once-transparent base became top-secret, and it restricted all community communication. The only time the base had any presence in the community was during the Cuban Missile Crisis. Sister Margaret Briody was a young nun in training in Amityville when the

Cuban Missile Crisis occurred in 1962. Sister Briody recalled: "Those were very tense times. People were very worried we might go to war. And during the Cuban Missile Crisis, uniformed soldiers could be seen rushing about, aiming 40-foot-long Nike antiaircraft missiles at the sky to be ready to shoot down any enemy bombers that might come."[129] These tensions came with concerns for the safety of the congested communities these bases were being operated in. Four years prior, a Nike base in New Jersey was performing daily safety checks on an arming device when an explosion killed ten workers. This explosion came after the army had assured the communities that the bases were as safe as a community gas station.[130] Accidents similar to the one in New Jersey were the catalysts that started the process of phasing out many of the bases. In the spring of 1971, locals around the remaining bases were shaken to their cores again. A Nike Hercules base in Sandy Hook, New Jersey, got reports of a stray Soviet bomber in American airspace and that sixteen missiles were pointed at the sky, ready to launch in seconds; all Long Island bases remained on alert.[131] Following the high-threat alerts and the community concerns over safety, the closure of these bases was further accelerated with Nixon's signing of the SALT agreement.

Cold War historian Donald Bender stated, "Long Island had a highly strategic location. It's near New York City and it juts out into the Atlantic Ocean, so if you're trying to stop an enemy aircraft, Long Island puts you out as far as you could go without getting your feet wet."[132] No nuclear-tipped missile was ever fired in war. Thus, by the "skin of our teeth" did Long Island avoid injury and death caused by nuclear detonations. The BOMARC base in Westhampton, today, is used by the Suffolk County government for storage, and the remaining area of the 186-acre site is now a shooting range for law enforcement officers. Today, this site stands as a relic of possible catastrophic threats caused by our own anxieties—if nuclear war had erupted.

8

AMERICA'S COLD WAR CONFLICTS BECOME WARS

Following the end of World War II, colonial powers were unable to afford the expense of defending overseas colonies. In addition to the costs, many of the colonies that had been shut off from the world by their colonial rulers for generations had global interaction during World War II. These emerging regions became the focus of the Soviet Union's and United States' fight for influence. In this fight of postwar global influence, the Korean and Vietnam Wars had the biggest effects on the state of New York. An estimated 482,000 New Yorkers served in the Korean War; 2,387 were killed in action. In the Vietnam War, an estimated 1 million New Yorkers served during the sixteen-year period, with 4,119 state residents killed. Despite the common belief that the Cold War was nothing more than a war of words, these international tensions, shaped local culture, trust in government, how we vote locally, communities collective mourning of its dead and emotional scared men and women.

The majority of Korean War soldiers were part of the silent generation, born between 1928 and 1945. In the shadow of the greatest generation, born between 1901 and 1927, who came to age during the Great Depression and fought in World War II, the silent generation came to age during the brutality of World War II. This generation was estimated to be composed of 55 million people throughout the country. The biggest generational gap in ideology was between the greatest generation and baby boomers. The baby boomers made up the generation born after World War II, between the years of 1946 and 1964. This generation was estimated to comprise 76 million people, and they were the first generation raised in most of Long Island's suburbs. The boomers were removed from the brutality of World War II and had a different interpretation of America's role in the world. But the biggest distinction between the two generations were their defining wars. The Korean War lasted three years, had strong backing from the United Nations and the public, did not rely heavily on a draft, was not televised much and the returning troops were welcomed back as heroes. In comparison, the Vietnam War, which lasted sixteen years, relied on the draft, had little pubic support, expanded into three countries without congressional consent due to the Gulf of Tonkin Resolution and the soldiers were not welcomed back with the same high morale. The boomers who fought in or witnessed the Vietnam War suffered unintended affects, which led to a budding counterculture. This counterculture made its way across Long Island in the form of antiwar views manicured through popular consumerism. But one of the biggest differences between World War II, the Korean War and the Vietnam War was the average age of the soldiers in active duty. During World War II and the Korean War, the average age for a soldier was twenty-six. During the Vietnam War, the average age of a soldier in combat was twenty-two. This four-year difference was a large gap, especially considering that the voting age was twenty-one until the passage of the Twenty-Sixth Amendment in 1971, which reduced the voting age to eighteen. This gap shaped political influence, engagement and perspectives of the two generations of combat soldiers. But the overall end result of the Vietnam War was 58,000 United States combat soldiers killed in action, an additional 3,000 missing in action and over 2 million dead South and North Vietnamese people.

Public opinion about the Vietnam War across Long Island originally was aligned with the elected officials' ability to shape the narrative of democracy versus communism, or, supposedly, good against evil. This policy was further fueled by the vestige of World War II–era patriotism that did not question authority. In Suffolk County, the anticommunist message resonated strongly, and during the election of 1964, between Lyndon Johnson and hardliner anticommunist Barry Goldwater, Goldwater received 44.37 percent of the vote, which was the highest percentage throughout the state. The following year, after Johnson escalated the war in Vietnam, a national Gallup poll reflected that 60 percent of Americans supported the escalation of the war, and 24 percent strongly opposed. Tensions and anxieties over communist threats were so high around this time that many Suffolk County locals believed the Soviets were invading from Montauk during the northeast blackout of November 1965. The overzealousness to fight communism among the World War II generation, at first, met limited resistance with the baby boomers, but as the draft was expanded, the boomers' opinions quickly shifted.

On June 8, 1956, United States Air Force sergeant Richard Bernard Fitzgibbon Jr. of Massachusetts was killed in Saigon, South Vietnam, by fellow airman Edward Clarke during a dispute. This story did not make headlines, and if it was covered, it was tucked away in the back pages of many newspapers. For many who read the about the death, it was their first insight into America's presence in the Indochinese country of Vietnam. Prior to the death of Fitzgibbon, most people in the United States had no knowledge that their country had had a presence in Vietnam since World War II. In July 1945, United States Army instructor Henry Prunler and six other men were parachuted into Vietnam. Their mission was to train a local militia called the Viet Minh on how to fight invading Japanese. When the war ended, the militia's alliance soured due to growing tensions between the ideology of communism and the Soviet Union. Two of the two hundred men trained by Prunler were Ho Chi Minh and Vo Nguyen Giap, who later became the leading forces against the United States. After the Korean War, the United States believed the solution was to contain communism by creating boarders, such as the thirty-eighth parallel between North and South Korea. In an attempt to beat back the communist influence, the United States would fight to create two countries, North and South Vietnam, divided by the seventeenth parallel. On February 6, 1963, Long Island had its first death in Vietnam. Air force major James Raymond O'Neil of Levittown was flying his B-26 over Pleiku Province, South Vietnam, to investigate the growing threat of communist guerrilla fighters called the Viet Cong. While in flight, the plane had engine trouble, and everyone except O'Neil was able to eject before crashing. This death was the first Long Island causality that got very little attention. Getting just as little attention were the details of the growing Viet Cong threat. The second death from Long Island occurred on May 6, 1963. Parker Dresser Cramer, an army first lieutenant and native of Wantagh, was killed by communist guerrillas in the Binh Duong Province of South Vietnam. Following the death, the U.S.-backed South Vietnamese first lady Madame Ngo Diah Nhu invited Cramer's parents and sister to her suite at the Hotel Barclay in New York to express her appreciation for Parker's service and condolences for his death.[133] On the heels of this visit was the death of marine corporal Charles Preston Tuthill of Uniondale. While over the Quang Nam Province of South Vietnam, Charles Tuthill died in a helicopter crash, the causes of which were described publicly as a

Corporal Charles Tuthill of Uniondale was one of the first Long Islanders killed in Vietnam. *Courtesy of the Tom and Jim Reece Vietnam Memorial.*

"non-crew"-related crash. These first three deaths across Long Island were announced with little to no attention through media outlets. Local media was covering the up-and-down trends of the local economy and Grumman's rebound in military defense sales of $7 million the upcoming year.

While U.S. deaths were on the rise, the presidency of Diem was in a freefall. Long-standing tensions between Vietnamese Buddhist and pro-Catholic policies were threating the stability of South Vietnam. The United States started to shift its support from Diem to his top general, Duong Van Minh, who would pave the way for a coup that killed Diem on November 2, 1963. This event set in motion a growing Viet-Cong threat. In response, Johnson signed the Gulf of Tonkin Resolution on August 10, 1964, which accelerated military operations. By 1966, the number of Long Islanders killed in Vietnam increased to forty-two. Within six months, that number would more than double to one hundred. Across Long Island, veterans of World War II viewed the military as a means of carrying on a proud military family tradition. Some other families and even local institutions believed the military would provide structure to youth with no clear direction after high school. These collective views kept a supply of young Long Islanders flowing into recruitment offices, which further added to the expansion of the number of drafted men in the army. Lee Allen of Uniondale would play army games on the streets with his friends; one group of kids were the Americans, and the other were the Koreans. But over a decade later, the childhood army games would become a reality. After dropping out of C.W. Post University, Lee was drafted on March 10, 1966. In July 1967, military operations heated up on the eve of Secretary of Defense McNamara's visit to Vietnam. McNamara, in his assessment of the operations, said, "The war was making progress, and more troops are needed." Lee was stationed outside of Long Binh, where he worked at Supply Depot 208. In the neighboring town six miles away, Ho Nai, Lee saw a country that was facing growing civil strife. An orphanage was set up for children whose parents were killed in the escalating conflict between North and South Vietnam. At night, Viet Cong would attack the town and take the boys from the orphanage in an effort to develop child soldiers. Following the attacks on the surrounding villages, the storage depots were fired on daily by light artillery from an almost invisible enemy recessed deep in the dense jungle.

Within two miles of Lee Allen's Uniondale home, George Motz of Garden City completed the ROTC program at Georgetown University. Upon completing his program, Motz was commissioned as a second lieutenant. Taking a break from his plans of earning a degree from Fordham University School of Law, George began his required military commitment. In March 1966, Motz was assigned to Charleston, South Carolina, as a survivor assistance officer.[134] His duties included reporting the death of a soldier killed during a deployment to their next-of-kin. Following his new assignment, Motz had to deliver the news to a mother about her son's death while he was on patrol in the Da Nang Province in Vietnam. The words weighed heavily with an understanding that he was about to destroy a family's way of life. A knock on the door, a woman greeting him with pleasantries and then the words: "The president of the United States, the Department of the Army and the People of the United States regret to inform you that your son died as a result of a gunshot wound to the head. He died at approximately 1700 hours on March 22 in Da Nang Province, Vietnam"[135] The reaction was everything he feared: crippling grief, a broken person trying to cope, pleas to God, a family traumatized and broken forever. Each week, these notifications increased, which reflected the brutal reality of a war that was escalating with no end in sight.

At the close of 1967, Long Island had an additional 120 soldiers killed within the year. Frank Romeo of Bay Shore and his friend decided to enlist in the United States Army after considering their options on the eve of their high school graduation. Frank, with his friend, enlisted at the United

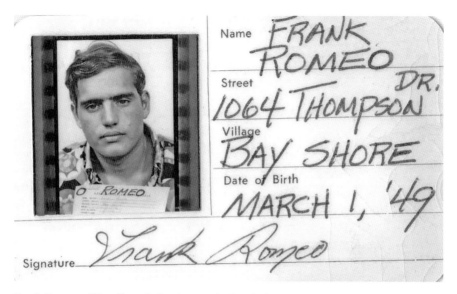

Frank Romeo of Bay Shore before he was deployed. *Courtesy of Frank Romeo.*

States Army Recruitment Office on Main Street in Bay Shore. When Frank enlisted, his thoughts of the United States as a force for good against the evils of communism dwarfed any fears of the unknown. Further selling Frank on the ideas of enlisting was the talk he had with St. Patrick's of Bay Shore's monsignor. The monsignor witnessed Frank's partying and advised him to join the army for structure and to serve a greater good.[136] Romeo recalled in later interviews, "Bay Shore class of 1967 had few choices: you could go to college and get a draft deferment, run to Canada to avoid any potential military service or stay local and run the risk of being drafted. This motivated at least 80 percent of the class to attempt college, even if they were not considered academic during their high school experience." After leaving bootcamp, Frank trained for the specialty unit 199th Infantry Brigade, which lived off the land and jumped into firefights from helicopters.

As the war was heating up, New York University freshman Jack Parente of Oyster Bay was falling behind academically. After flunking the spring semester of 1967, he was drafted. Following bootcamp, Parente signed up to take as many training programs as possible to delay being sent to Vietnam, but in December 1968, he was shipped out and assigned to United States Army, First Calvary.

In 1968, United States general Westmoreland was pushing for a tipping point, and North Vietnamese leaders were aggressively looking for a victory. From January 30 to September 23, 1968, the Tet Offensive stretched ground

Frank Romeo in Vietnam, where he was assigned to the 199th Infantry Brigade, 1968. *Courtesy of Frank Romeo.*

troops thin. By January 17, 474,300 men were on the ground in Vietnam, which was 1,500 more soldiers than the United States' peak strength in the Korean War, and by August, the troop numbers had grown to 541,000.[137] With the increased troop levels, the cost of war peaked to $25 billion. In early 1968, across Long Island, local district court judges started to utilize the option of having a youth defendant sign up for the service in exchange for avoiding jail time, probation or even for small violations. In April 1968, seventeen-year-old James Truex of Islip was being arraigned for a minor violation. During the arraignment, the judge recommended James to enlist in the army to provide him with a positive direction. James's father, a veteran of World War II and firm believer in the military, saw no other option for his son, who struggled academically in high school. Following his enlistment at

Jack Parente of Oyster Bay, who was assigned to the army's First Calvary during his deployment in Vietnam, 1969. *Courtesy of Jack Parente.*

Jack Parente while on deployment, bathing in a bomb crater contaminated with Agent Orange. The effects of the chemical were unknown to veterans until after the war. *Courtesy of Jack Parente.*

the United Sates Army Recruitment Office in Bay Shore, Truax was shipped out to first radio technician training, but motivated by the extra $51 a month in pay, he requested to be trained as a paratrooper.[138] Following training, Truax was assigned to the Eighty-Second Airborne.

As the headlines of all local newspapers reported large-scale escalation of the war in 1969, and with many branches of the military stretched thin, Bill Hughes of Bayside felt a sense of duty to do his part. When enlisting, Hughes believed he would become active in a communications unit, but he beat all expectations and was selected as a pararescue man for the United States Air Force. Hughes and the other men in the pararescue division had the responsibility of rescuing soldiers trapped behind enemy lines.

Claude Verga of East Meadow, inspired by stories of service to his country from his father, an army veteran who stormed the beaches of Normandy, signed up for the Coast Guard. Expecting to have more of a domestic role, his assigned cutter, the *Owasco*, was redeployed. Operation Market Time was an effort to stop supplies from South Vietnam flowing into North Vietnam. This operation became a priority as the war heated up in the late 1960s. In an effort to assist navy swift boats in searches of sampans, the Coast Guard sent in a limited number of cutters, including the *Owasco*, which was previously docked in New London, Connecticut.

At the close of 1968, Long Island lost an additional 160 soldiers, with 22 casualties in the month of May alone. The U.S. losses in Vietnam started to have many from the World War II generation question the country's commitment to its Cold War policy of communism containment. Weekly news stations started airing segments that covered live footage of the war, all centered on a different narrative than the one policy makers were spreading. The most damaging public image of the war was the medias' listing of soldiers killed daily. Locally, *Newsday* provided weekly summaries of the local soldiers killed, listing each branch, rank and hometown. With the coverage of battle-fatigued soldiers and daily causalities, the antiwar movement was trickling into Long Island from the counterculture antiwar demonstrations in New York City.

Nationally, politicians started taking stands that were more aggressive in their opposition to the war. A year prior, during the Democratic National Convention (DNC), protests over the lack of a unified antiwar platform evolved into riots on the streets of Chicago, near the convention. That November, Nixon came into office with the pledge to de-Americanize the war. Locally, the demonstrations became an opportunist platform for local- and state-elected officials. Democratic congressman Allard Lowenstein of Long

A pararescue team on alert in Vietnam; Bill Hughes *(far right)*. *Courtesy of Bill Hughes.*

Beach, during his reelection, took an aggressive antiwar stance and even frequented demonstrations to showcase his platform. New York Republican senator Charles Goodell surprised his constituents by showing up to a small antiwar demonstration at Hofstra University and publicly extended his support for peace in Vietnam. Nassau County executive Eugene Nickerson became vocal in his support of the protestors' antiwar stance, and he was a frequent guest at many of the growing antiwar demonstrations. On October 14, 1969, a nationwide antiwar protest was staged. Vietnam Moratorium Day had its first demonstration in the West Hempstead High School cafeteria in the form of an all-night vigil for fallen soldiers. The vigil quickly grew to include 600 people, including recently discharged veterans, who shared their stories and concerns about the direction of the war. Attendee

Claude Verga standing in front of his East Meadow home before being assigned to the
USCGC *Owasco*. *Courtesy of Claude Verga.*

and veteran Charles Guida of West Hempstead was asked if the war was
worth fighting. Guida replied, "Maybe the Second World War or Korea, but
not the Vietnam War. I went over with 65 guys, and 4 of us came back....
And for what? A lot of you think we're lucky we came back alive, but you're
wrong. We came back dead."[139] Another former soldier told the crowd that
the United States' and South Vietnam's vision did not reflect the majority
of Vietnamese people. Throughout the island communities, antiwar and
prowar demonstrations erupted. In Bay Shore, the Suffolk County Coalition
to End the War in Vietnam organized a march from South Shore Mall,
carrying cardboard coffin with the names of the 450 Long Islanders killed.[140]
The largest of these antiwar demonstrations were held in Eisenhower Park
East Meadow. Thousands gathered with signs in hand, reading "Peace
Now!" As the crowds grew, local folk singers preformed in the band shell,
and in between music sets, several speakers expressed views of dissent
relating to the war. Prowar demonstrations and counterdemonstrations were
staged by several groups, but the most extreme were the local chapters of

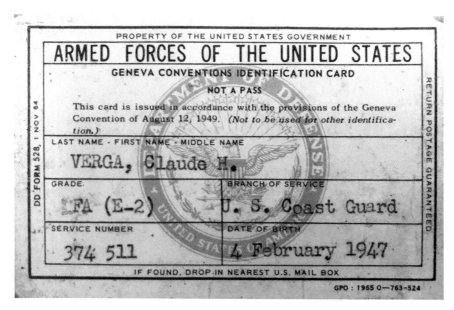

The *Owasco* and its crew were assigned to Vietnam to participate Operation Market Time to disrupt the supply lines of the North Vietnamese. Pictured is the Geneva Convention card that was issued to armed forces going into combat. *Courtesy of Claude Verga.*

Left: Claude Verga (the author's father) in Vietnam in the summer of 1968. *Courtesy of Claude Verga.*

Right: Harold Mason of Hempstead was killed in 1968, near the Binh Thuan Providence. *Courtesy of the Tom and Jim Reece Vietnam Memorial.*

the Long Island Ku Klux Klan. Marching in the streets of Ronkonkoma, the Klan held signs affirming their anticommunist stance. Following Vietnam Moratorium Day, the demonstrations continued and spread into almost every high school, college and university throughout the Long Island region.

On November 14, 1969, the one thousandth soldier from Queens, Nassau and Suffolk was killed. In a tribute to the soldiers lost, one thousand black balloons were released by the Nassau County Executive Offices in Garden City. In addition to the higher mortality rate of Long Island, the My Lai Massacre made it into headlines after over a year of trying to keep it from the press. The massacre of an estimated five hundred unarmed

Nicholas Fritz of Brentwood was killed in 1968, near the Thua Thien Providenc, *Courtesy of Joe Fritz.*

Vietnamese civilians became another target for mass demonstrations. Students for a Democratic Society established chapters at Stony Brook University, Nassau Community College and Adelphi University. With the newest chain of events at the close of 1969, protests became more aggressive and, in many cases, antimilitary. These protests were in strong contrast to the peaceful "bring the soldiers home" picketing.

While the antiwar movement was heating up throughout Long Island, the military's efforts on the ground started to become compromised. Drug use among soldiers was on the rise, and racial tensions among soldiers were escalating. James Truax recalls "some medics that were Hispanic or southern White would walk over injured Black soldiers, or sometimes withhold penicillin from Black soldiers that contracted STDs from their time on leave. These actions instigated brawls among racial clichés, but despite the tensions, the men still maintained unity during the thick of the fight." Other challenges were the Americans' movements on the ground becoming almost routine. Truax recalled, "We would get our orders to be sent out and not know where we were going, but when we got there, the local Vietnamese barbers and prostitutes from the night before in the last town were there before us."

Amid these internal conflicts, in the spring of 1970, troops were starting to be sent to Cambodia, near the Kampong Cham Providence, often referred to as the "Fishhook." Frank Romeo was assigned to track enemy base camps up into Cambodia. During a mission in Cambodia, Romeo's division had supplies dropped a mile away and were going into their second day with no food and water in the humid, dense jungle. Refusing to give up their hard-fought gained territory, the division went to retrieve the supplies and had Romero stay to defend the line. Moments later, he was ambushed by Viet Cong and woke up a month later in a military hospital.

While moving into Cambodia, Bill Hughes and fellow air rescue crews were sent on a series of missions into North Vietnam and Laos. While attempting to rescue a pilot in Laos, Hughes and his fellow air rescuer recalled, one night, coming through Mu Gia Pass (a mountain range through Laos and North Vietnam) with the lights of the helicopter off to avoid being identified by a heavily armed Viet Minh line. "While checking the fuel, the helicopter pilot hit the wrong switch and turned the lights on to the aircraft. Within seconds, the sky lit up with antiaircraft munitions, but luckily, hours later, traversing the pass, the aircraft landed safely back at the home base."[141]

In April 1970, at Hofstra University's Weller Hall, the Student Mobilization Committee staged a sit-in for over twelve hours. Their demands were that the ROTC program on the campus be discontinued. The protest was ended when State Supreme Court Justice Bernard Meyer issued an order to end the sit-in.[142] After meetings that followed the protest between Hofstra vice-president William Heston and Student Mobilization Committee president Norman Coleman, an agreement was reached for more student input in the administration's decisions relating to the campus's operations. This sit-in would be overshadowed by the demonstrations and shutdowns to come in the following months. On May 4, 1970, at Kent State University in Ohio, a student protest and occupation over America's expansion into Cambodia turned deadly. The national guard was called in to break up the protest, and as a result, four students were killed, and nine were injured. Two days later, on May 6, C.W. Post, Dowling, Hofstra University, Nassau Community and Suffolk Community Colleges suspended classes due to collective student sit-ins and occupations

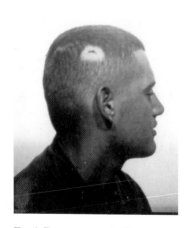

Frank Romeo, near the Kampong Cham Providence in Cambodia, was ambushed. Pictured is an injury to Frank's head. *Courtesy of Frank Romeo.*

of administration buildings. These demonstrations were done in an effort to show solidarity with the Kent State shooting victims and protest the United States' expansion into Cambodia. Adelphi, Farmingdale College, and New York Institute of Technology held occupations and demonstrations but did not suspend classes. At Stony Brook University, nine hundred demonstrators turned destructive. Firebombs were detonated at the Tabler Dormitory, humanities building and groundskeeping facilities. Branching off from the campus, demonstrators had carpooled and descended on Smithtown's Main Street draft board. When they arrived at the draft board, the protesters were met with two hundred police officers in full riot gear surrounding the building. As the students demonstrated, drivers who attempted to drive through the densely crowded streets had their windows broken by the protesters.[143] By 12:30 a.m., the protest had dispersed with little to no arrests. A total of eight hundred students and faculty had to be evacuated before that section of the campus had its fires under control. Classes were able to resume the following day. In Port Washington, Syosset, Plainview, Harborfields and West Islip High Schools, students held organized mass rallies against the Kent State shooting and the expansion of the war. Thousands of high school students in these communities refused to attend classes and took the demonstrations into their communities. By May 12, all classes had resumed in every Long Island college, university and high school.

By mid-1973, America's involvement in the war was winding down. In March, the United States and North Vietnam agreed on ending all direct American military operations. Almost every community across Long Island had at least a couple of causalities from the war. Levittown had the most losses in the war, a total of 21 killed in action (KIA). For the most part, many veterans came home quietly, with no victory parade. In Uniondale, 10 of the 141 who had gone off to Vietnam were killed. On April 30, 1975, South Vietnam was invaded, Saigon fell to the North Vietnamese and the unification of Vietnam as a communist state marked the United States' failure of containment, which further lowered morale for soldiers. Sergeant Richard Perricone of Uniondale, who was taken as a prisoner of war in 1967, was released by Viet Cong forces in 1973. In an effort to build morale for the local soldiers returning home and to honor the ones lost, the town of Uniondale organized a "welcome home, Richard" celebration. An estimated 8,000 to 10,000 people lined the street as the brown sedan carrying Richard went down Jerusalem Avenue.[144] American flags were in full display throughout every store and almost every home in the town. Most returning POWs and soldiers had no celebration. POW Sergeant

This page: A student protest at Hofstra University. This 1970 protest was an antiwar and civil rights protest. Part of the student protest was organized by Student Mobilization Committee, which staged a sit-in at Weller Hall. *Courtesy of Hofstra University, Special Collections.*

Arthur Cormier of Bay Shore was held prisoner along with future Arizona senator John McCain. Many locals did not even know when he was released from the Viet Cong or when he returned home. The community of Bay Shore/North Bay Shore had lost twelve, but soldiers such as Romero, who came home after a year in the hospital, became an emotional casualty. Romero recalled, "Coming home to Bay Shore, the community tried to be supportive; my parents tried to help but were unable. I see someone get vaporized by stepping on a land mine, and I became addicted to drugs due to the year on morphine while in the hospital; they could not help." Making Romeo's struggle even more challenging was the resentment returning soldiers witnessed outside of Bay Shore. While Romero was in a wheelchair, an antiwar protester spit on him. James Truax had similar struggles after returning home. Truax was discharged in Oakland, California, and took a plane back to New York. After being discharged, Truax had not slept for more than twenty-four hours, so he slept on the flight. Once the plane landed, he woke up to an empty plane; the staff told him, "They were scared to wake him, not knowing how he would respond." When arriving in Islip, Truax's drinking habit crossed to the level of alcoholism, and soon, he became a fixture at the Islip bar Hutleys (now Maxwells on Main Street). Truax expressed, "People seemed more distant when I got home; the town looked the same, but people were not." After returning to Long Island in 1970, Jack Parente was surprised to find a divide among World War II veterans and the Vietnam veterans. AMVETS Post bars and other AMVETS social events that would have World War II vets in attendance referred to their war as the "real war" when trying to draw comparisons between their experiences and those of the Vietnam veterans.[145] Jack, half joking, further explained, "Being a Vietnam vet came with a stigma, but it got a little better around the time *Rambo* the movie came out." When Bill Hughes returned home in 1974, he dressed in his full military uniform with a chest full of metals, feeling a strong sense of accomplishment for all the soldiers' lives he'd saved. While he disembarked from the plane at La Guardia Airport, an antiwar protestor cursed at him and spit on him. To Hughes's surprise, these attacks and verbal assaults were common toward veterans coming home, which, to this day, affects Hughes every time he sees a peace symbol.[146]

Despite his struggles, Romeo was able to get back on his feet and opened a catering hall, and Truax had a long career as a line man for LICO/LIPA. Bill Hughes attempted civilian life but rejoined the service and became a founding member of the 106th Rescue Group, New York Air National

Guard pararescue team. This team rescued countless sailors off the coast of Long Island and in the Northern Atlantic. On one 1977 mission with the new pararescue team, Hughes was sent to a distressed Soviet spy boat off the coast of Long Island. On the boat, one of the crew members was having an appendicitis attack. Before being sent aboard the spy ship, Hughes and his fellow team members prepared a peace offering that included a stack of *Playboy* magazines for the Soviets. When the rescue was completed, the men at the base joked, "This mission and peace offering would be the first détente of the Soviets and Americans." It may not have been a détente in reality, but it was an example of the thawing tensions between United States and the Soviets.

As the 1970s drew to a close, the public's fears of communism evolved. By the close of the Vietnam War, public concerns shifted from nuclear war to economic stagflation or a gas shortage. The public demanded a shift in governmental priorities. The other shift in views surrounded the policy of containment as a weapon. The Vietnam War reflected the weaknesses of this policy but pushed the United States to normalize its relationship with China, a long-standing ally of the Soviet Union. But the largest impact of the war was the government's neglect and the public's stigma of the Vietnam veteran that endured for the coming decade. Antiwar demonstrators, in many cases, took their frustrations with United States' policies in Vietnam out on returning soldiers. Soldiers were also referred to as crazy or baby killers, which socially isolated many of them. In 1975, the emotions of the returning soldiers and the loss of South Vietnam to North Vietnam delayed any city homecoming parade.

Decades later, Bill Hughes became a founding member of the 106th Rescue Group, New York Air National Guard, and the West Hampton VFW Post 5350 Commander. *Courtesy of Bill Hughes.*

In an effort for local communities to pay tribute to the soldiers who were killed, Wyandanch renamed an elementary school for local resident La Francis Hardiman of the 173rd Airborne. While on a patrol, Hardiman's company was ambushed, and he was killed in November 1967. In Hempstead, Harold Mason had memories of walking his daughter in a stroller through a Hempstead Village park not far from his house. Mason enlisted in the

To honor Harold Mason, Hempstead Village renamed a park not far from his house Harold Mason Park. Pictured is Harold's daughter on the swing and his mother standing next to his daughter, holding flowers. *Courtesy of the Hempstead Public Library.*

army and was sent to Vietnam, but in 1968, he was killed in an ambush in the Binh Thuan Providence. Years following his death, the park his daughter visited was renamed to honor her father. As for the surviving veterans, ten years later, on May 7, 1985, under Mayor Edward Koch, they received their traditional ticker tape homecoming parade.

9

ERODED TRUST AND THE RISE
OF LONG ISLAND'S RUST BELT

By the mid-1970s and into the mid-1980s, postwar suburbia was entering its middle ages. While the region aged, its naive blind faith in the government became a nostalgic pastime. According to a Pew research poll, by 1975, only 25 percent of Americans trusted the government. This number was a sharp decline from 1964, when the same poll reflected that 77 percent trusted the government. In a little over a decade, the Vietnam War escalated, causing mass casualties through flawed policy; the United States was also still in the shadow of Nixon's Watergate Scandal, and the government's domestic spying operations became public. Congressional candidates used this public sentiment as a backboard for inquiry hearings into the overreach of the government's powers and accountability for failed policies.

LONG ISLAND OFFICIALS QUESTION AUTHORITY

Otis Pike, a Democrat congressman from Suffolk County and New York's First District (this district included Brookhaven, Smithtown, Southold, Southampton, East Hamptons, Islip, Riverhead and Shelter Island), was a U.S. Marine veteran who got attention locally for sponsoring a bill to make Fire Island a national seashore in 1964. One of the fastest-growing regions in the Unites States, Pike's district had a large and growing population of

Vietnam veterans. By 1972, many of his constituents had growing concerns about a war with no end in sight. Pike was one of the first congressman to call out the air force's unauthorized bombing campaigns in North Vietnam under the command of General Lavelle. Following the public inquiry, General Lavelle stepped down from his post and did not maintain his rank of major general, but he did maintain a lower rank, lieutenant general. The Nixon administration did not directly admit that it gave authorization for the bombing campaign. Perplexed, Pike described the response as a "curve ball" from the Nixon cabinet.

The coming December, in 1974, CIA operations against counterculture groups became front-page news. This triggered the newly appointed president Gerald Ford to form a committee to explore the use of the CIA in domestic spying. Selected to head the committee was Otis Pike, who had the vague focus of exploring CIA abuses of power at the taxpayers' expense. Exploring the budget, Pike discovered that intelligence spending was four times larger than what Congress was told. While following the money, domestic spying was not the only abuse of power—there were also possible assassinations of international leaders. Further exploring the money trail, Pike subpoenaed files from the intelligence community's involvement in the Tet Offensive in 1968. This request ended all cooperation between the president and Congress. During the investigation, Pike felt the CIA started domestic spying operations on him to destroy his credibility.[147] In a memo to Chief of Staff Donald Rumsfeld from Secretary of the Cabinet Jim Connor, Conner stated, "Pike has latched onto the issue and is using it as a platform for political ambitions. There is no evidence that he will act responsibly or will retrain efforts to preserve the function of the intelligence community. All efforts to negotiate with Pike as to what is declassified have failed."[148] In a call to Pike, James Reston, a columnist and former executive editor of *New York Times*, complained about his committee's investigation and told Pike, "What are you guys doing down there?" This call affirmed to Pike the attitude of the mainstream press toward the committee. To save face in the hearings, CIA agents who were witnesses to the committee affirmed that there would be no disclosure of any further classified information and no testimonies concerning classified information—unless the president certified the material was declassified.[149] This action effectively killed the investigation and following the end of the investigation, the House of Representatives convened and voted 246 to 124 to not the release the Pike Committee Report. Out of frustration, Pike called journalist Karl Grossman to discuss the suppression of the report. Grossman suggested to Pike that it should surface in the press; Grossman told Pike that "it is a right to know issue." During the call, it was suggested that the report get to the *Village Voice* for publication. The report of the Pike Committee was published in the *Village Voice*, and it detailed important conclusions that the CIA was not a "rogue elephant" but, as it declared, "all evidence in hand suggests that the CIA, far from being out of control, has been utterly responsive to the instructions of the president and the assistant to the president for National Security Affairs."[150] Other findings in the report cited that the CIA was posing as journalists in more than fifteen news organizations. This publication cemented Pike's congressional legacy of fighting the intelligence agencies' overreach of power. After the report was published Grossman and Pike met up in a tavern on Main Street in Riverhead. Pike explained his frustration with Congress not allowing the release of the report and the lack of support in mainstream media. The resistance in releasing the report spurred him to consider a career in the press. Grossman suggested that Pike contact Dave Starr, the editor of the *Long Island Press* and national editor of the *Newhouse Newspaper* chain. Starr was Grossmans's editor at the *Long Island Press*. Pike spoke to Starr, and Starr offered Pike a column that was syndicated nationally by the Washington-based Newhouse News Service that Starr oversaw. Pike's column would run for over twenty years.

With Pike's crusades against the CIA's abuse of power, two Long Islanders would become the examples of intelligence community corruption that was birthed from a culture of limited to unchecked power. CIA director William Casey of Roslyn Harbor had a laundry list of scandals that became public. The most publicized of these scandals involved insider trading, or what some would consider stock price manipulation. While using CIA operations, Casey bet against companies on the stock exchange, knowing how the secret operations would affect induvial companies. An example of this occurred when his agency received intelligence about growing tensions between Libya and Saudi Arabia, which pushed him to invest in oil stocks; this also occurred when CIA spies found out about Japan's development of a new microchip, which was speculated to have pushed Casey to buy Japanese company stock in Sony.[151] In Casey's first year as CIA director, in 1981, he reported $442,000 on the sales of forty-five stocks that were believed to be determined off American intelligence paid for by the taxpayer. Other CIA officials accused in the insider trading allegations was one-time East Hills resident Max Hugel, the head of Clandestine Service. Hugel resigned to avoid further congressional hearings over his finances. As the stock scandal played out in the headlines, Cassy was brought up on chargers for a 1976 (before he officially became a CIA director) violation of the agents' registration law. He violated this law by representing the government of Indonesia in meetings at Treasury Secretary William Simon's Hamptons residence over tax policies that affected oil companies that traded with Indonesia.[152] With all these charges against the director, President Reagan announced his confidence in Casey and stated he would not ask him to resign. With a combination of Pike's congressional hearings, the scandals of Casey's leadership and the lack of accountability for the scandals within a decade, the agencies' reputations were damaged for decades to come.

"I Died in Vietnam and Did Not Know It"

Frank McCarthy, a Vietnam veteran, traveled out to Patchogue, Suffolk County, in the early hours of the morning, looking for a lawyer named Victor Yannacone. Once he arrived at his Baker Street, Patchogue office, Frank was disappointed to find out Yannacone was on an extended weekend break to celebrate his wedding anniversary. Having prior knowledge that Yannacone had an interest in filing a suit against an herbicide company made Frank's journey a necessity. Yannacone shelved the potential herbicide suit not only due to a lack of participating law firms but because the DDT legal war he waged years prior yielded little to no return for his overhead. Refusing to wait for when the office would open, Frank spent the night camped out in his car, waiting for morning to confront Yannacone at his home. This was going to be his friend Paul Reutershan's last mission. Reutershan was suffering the effects of pancreatic cancer and was unable to carry out his last request of holding someone accountable for what had happened to veterans like him, who had increasing amounts of obscure illnesses. Noticing someone camped out near his driveway, Yannacone went outside to confront McCarthy. McCarthy stared down Yannacone, almost at a loss for words, and said, "Please, you have to help my friend Paul Reutershan."[153] McCarthy went on to explain that Reutershan, Jimmy Sparrow and himself formed the Vietnam Veterans Agent Orange Victims advocate group. Collectively, the three were advocating for veterans suffering from cancer or who had children with birth defects; they wanted justice for their prolonged exposure to the dioxin-based chemical Agent Orange, which they felt was the cause of their troubles. An estimated 12 to 20 million gallons of Agent Orange was sprayed in Vietnam in order to destroy the dense jungle and limit Viet Cong ambushes, but veterans were exposed with no protection while dispersing this dioxin-based chemical. Based on his success with the Environmental Defense Fund, which banned DDT and set the standard for environmental law, Yannacone's help would be essential for the advocate group's success. McCarthy further explained that a portion of the estimated 2.4 million veterans who were dually certified healthy by two medical agencies to go to war and documented as some of the healthiest men in the United States started to die in less than a decade from old-age diseases.[154] In addition to old-age illnesses, veterans were experiencing an increasing number of their children being born with spina bifida, other physical birth defects and various neurological disorders. Yannacone explained that he was done fighting these big battles, such as the DDT war, but McCarthy refused to leave and take no as an answer. Inspired by his determination, and after consulting his family, Yannacone again decided to take on a giant. Giving McCarthy a cup of coffee and a legal pad, he asked him to write down what he would want to achieve in this case. While writing, Yannacone was taken back by his objectives:

- Veterans need medical care and treatment for their family members effected by their exposure to Agent Orange.
- Veterans do not want to be recipients of public assistance and feel it is not the burden of the taxpayer to cover medical expenses. These expenses are the responsibilities of the herbicide manufacturers.
- Veterans and their families seek to test those safety claims of the corporate defendants in the crucible of cross-examination before a court of equity, not in administrative proceedings, which can drag on for decades.
- Veterans seek punitive damages against the corporate defendant war contractors responsible for the advertising, promotion, marketing and sale of phenoxy herbicides contaminated with toxic synthetic organic chemicals, such as the polychlorinated dibenzo-p-dioxins (PCDDs) and the polychlorinated dibenzo furans (PCDFs) in an amount sufficient to convince corporate management they serve as trustees of the public health, safety and welfare to an extent commensurate with the economic power and technological resources of the corporations they manage.[155]

McCarthy then went on to explain that, overall, this was an example of how the Vietnam combat veterans were treated—"lower than whale shit, which was oceans and oceans deep." With all the objectives listed and the brief conversation, Yannacone understood that this was not just a battle for compensation but a mandate to restore the dignity and honor of Vietnam veterans.

A suit was quickly filed against eight makers of Agent Orange for billions of dollars. The defendant companies included Dow Chemical, Monsanto Company, Diamond Shamrock, Uniroyal Inc., T.H. Agriculture, Nutrition Company, Hercules Inc. and Thompson Chemical Company in the Federal Southern District Court in Brooklyn. That evening, Yannacone's phone ran off the hook with calls from as far as Australia and Canada.

Lawyer Victor Yannacone filed lawsuits against the chemical companies that produced Agent Orange, which affected hundreds of thousands Vietnam veterans. *Courtesy of Victor Yannacone.*

All of the callers were reporting similar stories of Vietnam veterans with cancer or having children with severe birth defects. Following the filed suit, environmental lawyer and Bay Shore resident Irving Like joined the growing litigation. Like established himself as the lawyer who helped get Fire Island preserved as a national seashore and who fought the opening of Shoreham Nuclear Power Plant. His experience would not only strengthen the lawsuit against the companies, but it would expand the suit into federal government liability. The cause of the legal argument against the companies was "failure to warn," even with knowledge of the product's dangers. The defending companies quickly formed a legal argument that the government and the companies had no knowledge of the affects and that they had government contractor immunity from prosecution. In March 1979, the trail was set in the U.S. District Court in Westbury, and George Pratt became the presiding judge over the case. Westbury was picked due to the 260 plaintiffs who were from the New York tristate area. Days prior to the trial, *Newsday* highlighted some of the local residents who had children suffering from the birth defects due to their exposure to Agent Orange.

Plaintiff Michael Ryan of Stony Brook, served in 1967 but, years later, had a daughter born with spine malformed, missing bone in her right arm,

*several missing figures, cleft palate and a large hole in her heart. Plaintiff
Guy Salvio of Rocky Point had his son born missing internal tissue and
a cleft palate, and Robert Fennessey from Suffolk County had his daughter
die three days before the birth. The autopsy revealed massive birth defects as
the cause of the miscarriage.*[156]

On March 21, hundreds of veterans and their families crowded into
a Westbury courtroom with similar stories. This trial was the first in a
series of trials that continued until 1984. This hearing was over whether
the jurisdiction of the case would be considered federal and under the
Environmental Protection Agency (EPA). United States marshals stood
guard around the building and in the court room, armed with semiautomatic
guns as a precaution against any threats. Victor Yannacone, in an interview
reflecting on the tone of the room, stated:

*When Judge Pratt came into the room, before the clerk said all rise, a
veteran in his marine uniform from the back of the room yelled, "A ten-
hut," and all the veterans stood at attention until the judge took his seat.
Another man stood at attention after everyone was seated with the American
flag. The defense lawyer asked the court clerk to have the soldier take the flag
down and sit. The judge, noticing the escalating conflict, asked the clerk,
"What is the problem?"*

*The clerk replied, "He is not lowering the flag." In response, the judge
said, "This is an American courtroom; the flag stays."*

While reassessing the environment of the courtroom and noticing the
dozens of the children present suffering from birth defects, Pratt ordered the
clerks to set the parents up in the jury room with wired audio of the court in
an effort to make them more confrontable.

On August 15, 1979, Judge Pratt ruled that the EPA, not the courts, should
make the decision to "allegedly serious environmental hazards of Agent
Orange and ordered the defendant companies to make no further dilatory
procedural motions that would further delay the suit.[157] The next stop was
the U.S. District Court in Brooklyn. The presiding judge was Jack Weinstein,
a veteran of World War II. Once in Brooklyn, Keith Kavanagh, a law
partner to Yannacone, brought his background in science to the courtroom.
Kavanagh detailed 2,4,5-T, the toxic ingredient in Agent Orange, by using
various visual models. By the time the case reached its final trial date in early
1984, the number of plaintiffs had grown to over 20,000. Agent Orange

veterans' advocate James Sparrow stated in interviews, "We expanded the number of plaintiffs through media, 24-hour help lines and having it posted in every VFW hall."[158] With the growing number of claims, lawyer Leonard Rivkin of Garden City joined the plaintiff's legal team. On May 7, a settlement was reached between the chemical companies and the growing number of 150,000 plaintiffs. The final settlement number was $180 million, with $61,000 a day in interest. In an interview about the future of the suit, Irving Like stated, "Now that this is resolved, we can turn our attention to the government."[159] For many veterans across Long Island, this disregard for soldiers and their families would echo Vietnam veterans' sentiment that was best summed up by Paul Reutershan, who said before the start of the suit, "I died in Vietnam but didn't even know it."

Long Island's Rust Belt

In the late 1970s and early 1980s, the cooling of Cold War tensions sent many of the defense plants into an economic tailspin. The once-proud military high-end production that many towns across the island prided themselves on were all facing aggressive restructuring as a last-ditch effort to be profitable. In the 1970s, following the SALT agreement, Grumman attempted to break into a civilian market. In the early 1980s, Grumman employed an estimated thirty-five thousand people in its manufacturing plants and other various small-scale local subcontractor companies. Grumman spent millions on the tracked levitation research vehicle (TLRV), which had a high speed of three hundred miles per hour. This breakthrough one-track rail system was not embraced. To raise money for the loss in experimental projects and sharp reduction in military contracts, Grumman sold off 80 percent of its domestic jet manufacturing subsidiary Grumman American Aviation to American Jet Industry. The sale of this subsidiary created Gulfstream American Corporation. This sale had no effect on Long Island jobs but became an indicator of the direction Grumman officials felt would be a lifeline to fix other economic woes. By 1979, Grumman's profits were off by 38 percent, and their only profitable big-ticket item was the F-14, which had slowed in orders. Worse for Grumman was that it was caught in middle of scandal, as it had sold 80 of its F-14s to the Iranian army, which was then in the hands of the Ayatollah and Republican Guard following the overthrow of the Sha. In addition to Grumman getting caught in the illegal arms sale, its subsidiary Gulfstream was fined for fraud, as it had used agents for Gulf Stream sales in Bahrain to blur the trail of Iran's $1.5 billion for the F-14s. In an effort to diversify products, smaller-ticketed items such as the Grumman LLV truck were remarketed. This truck was exclusively made for the United States Postal Service. The assembly of these trucks was later removed from Long Island facilities to Montgomery, Pennsylvania. But the largest mass-produced nonmilitary product was Grumman's buses. Each bus was marketed and sold across all cities in America for $145,000 each. But this product had its setbacks. Of the 870 busses that were bought by New York City and the MTA, 637 had to be withdrawn from service within the first six months.[160] The safety issues with the busses were related to cracks on the frames and undercarriages. This problem came in the middle of a $30 million contract for an additional 500 buses. Blame was quickly shifted to Grumman subcontractor Flxible. Despite promises to repair the issue, the MTA asked Grumman to withdraw from the additional bid for the 500 buses. This was the beginning of major image problems for Grumman Corporation. Observing Grumman's weaknesses being played out in the media, the Texas-based firm LTV Corporation offered the company $450 million, or $0.70 per each share. In a move to prevent a buyout or aggressive takeover, Grumman sought out a majority of the 14,100,000 shares. To prevent a takeover, Grumman would have to get 7.1 million shares for majority control. As of October 1981, Grumman had 5,330,600 shares in the hands of the board of directors and employee investment plans. Grumman set a goal of buying back 1 million shares and then another 769,000 shares.

In 1983, the Reagan administration set up the Strategic Defense Initiative Organization, commonly referred to as "Star Wars." This initiative was proposed as a missile system around the United States through satellites that would have the ability to shoot any incoming warheads. In reality, the initiative only caused an increase in defense spending. This additional spending amounted an estimated $4.9 billion in funding for potential Grumman contracts. The F-14D was under development; it had an updated radar system with a new infrared tracker system. This potential lifeline for Grumman would be short term; the company was hemorrhaging money again in 1985. In the fall of 1985, Fairchild Republic got its T-46A jet trainer program canceled. The cancellation came after a defense budget cut, which Long Island resident and senator Alfonse D'Amato attempted to filibuster for four hours.[161] In an interview, Congressman Thomas Downey of Amityville said, "We battled this cut with every ounce of our strength, but nothing is powerful as the senate opposition from Senator Goldwater."

The Fairchild Republic
T-46A jet trainer was
canceled by the Defense
Department in 1985.
This contract cancellation
led to the closing of
the Republic Plant in
Farmingdale. *Courtesy of the
U.S. Air Force Museum.*

Goldwater and other senators were concerned about the $3 billion price tag that they collectively evoked the Gramm-Rudman Deficit Reduction Law to stop the contract. The Gramm-Rudman Deficit Reduction Law was set in place in 1985 to reduce the national deficit.

With this loss, Fairchild Republic was forced to close its manufacturing plant in Farmingdale, laying off over 3,500 workers. The debt of the company was $279 million, and with the canceling of the contract, the stock dropped to an all-time low of $13.25 share.[162] In a last-ditch effort to save Fairchild Republic, the manufacturing subsidiary was offered to Grumman for a fire sale of a price. The plant was marketed as an opportunity to combine future military contracts. In response to the pleas of the fifty-six-year-old firm, Grumman declined the offer, stating, "The acquisition would place too great a demand on financial and technical resources."[163] Many corporate analysts believed the real reason why Grumman did not buy Fairchild Republic was that it was unionized and Grumman was not. In March 1987, the formerly vibrant firm that had constructed such planes as the P-47 Thunderbolt and once had the title of the "Arsenal of Democracy" bestowed on it during World War II closed its doors for good. On its final day, Vincent Damiano, a general manger who spent thirty-seven and a half years with the company, somberly gathered his belongings. When confronted by a reporter and asked about the closing, he said, "They just walked around and told us and…it's unbelievable."[164]

In early 1989, much of the allocated funding for the F-14D was drying up, and a cancellation of the upcoming year's contract was proposed. A total cut of $1.3 billion was proposed that included the $295 million for the Grumman F-14D. This would affect the 5,600 Long Islanders on the development team. The proposed cut shook up many projects, but at the last minute, funding was preserved. It became clear for many workers and shareholders that Grumman was living contract to contract, and with one canceled contract, the firm would become like Fairchild Republic. At Christmastime in 1989, employees were expecting a great holiday with their families, but instead, 10 percent of all employees received layoff notices. A total of 3,100 people were laid off, which added to the 1,800 people who were laid off just a year prior. The layoffs accelerated, and in late December 1991, the Soviet Union declared that it would cease operations as a country. On July 1992, the last F-14 came out of Calverton Airfield. This marked the end of the largest Cold War military airplane program on Long Island.[165] The F-14 Tomcat, program employed 15 percent of all Grumman workers. Promises that the employees of the program would not be laid off but transferred to maintenance and support were quickly broken. These cuts added to Long Island's growing unemployment statistic. The end of production and the Cold War became the end of a military manufacturing industry throughout Long Island. The Grumman Corporation reduced its workers from just under 30,000 in 1992 to 10,500 in 1993. The Great River Grumman Electronics Plant announced that it would close its doors by the summer of 1993, which would leave the local school district of East Islip missing $503,906 a year in lost tax revenue. The town of Islip would suffer $71,000 in lost tax revenue—and this number grew each year. The East Islip School District would go under an austerity budget until the property could go back on the tax rolls. This budget crunch would affect 4,400 student sports and art programs for the next five years. The shopping plazas in and around the town quickly became vacant, which added to the city's lost revenue. For Grumman, the only concern was to be more profitable in the short term and marketable for a merger. By 1994, the island's last large military manufacturer was sold off to Northrop Corporation. The final sales price was $2.11 billion; more than two-thirds of the company's stocks were bought up in an effort to give Northrop a 90 percent majority. Once Northrop got 90 percent of the shares, it was able to lock out other Grumman shareholders from meetings. This was the beginning of an aggressive de-Grummanization of Long Island. As the employees were reduced from 34,000 to 22,000 and then to 9,000, all of the surrounding communities quickly started to have much of their shopping plazas become vacant. Lost tax revenue snowballed, and many towns and school districts, similar to East Islip, faced steep cutbacks. Many towns quickly rezoned the industrial sites to become residential to get them back on the tax rolls, but despite these efforts, the expenses of operating the local school systems fell solely on the homeowner. With no industrial tax base, residential school taxes skyrocketed.

Shifts in tax burdens, slowly dying retail centers and growing unemployment were not the only devastations Long Island faced. By the early 1960s, the groundwater in Nassau and Suffolk Counties was showing signs of contamination from industrial sites. The counties' water supply came from a series of underground aquifers that are replenished through rainwater and are vulnerable to contaminants. By the time the defense manufacturing plants had left, the island the system was overwhelmed, and pollution was rampant, due, in part, to industries not properly disposing of chemicals. When Grumman, Republic and their subcontractors closed or left Long Island, the Environmental Protection Agency (EPA) designated 250 "superfund toxic-waste sites." Between the counties, Suffolk had 109 and Nassau 145 superfund sites. Water contamination represented 90 percent of all the island's designated sites. The most common chemical in all these sites was the carcinogen tetrachloroethylene, or PCE. The four most polluted sites were Lake Success, the Sperry/Lockheed Martin Plant, the Brookhaven National Laboratory, the Calverton Grumman Plant, and the Bethpage Grumman Plant.

In the mid-1990s, the water authority under the old Sperry factory in Lake Success discovered a plume of toxic chemicals. The Sperry site, which comprised ninety-four acres, had a chemical plume the size of nine hundred acres between one hundred and four hundred feet underground. The plume included three main cancer-causing chemicals: trichloroethene (TCE), tetrachloroethene (PCE) and dichloroethene (DCE). For years, Sperry was dumping chemicals from its factory into drywells, but they leaked into to the local water table. To do the cleanup, the cost would total more than $97 million, take over thirty years and require the construction of extraction wells. From 1995 to May 2013, Sperry/Lockheed Martin fought the state's Department of Environmental Conservation (DEC) over paying the costs of a full cleanup. The final settlement was that the company would cover $25 million and the state and county taxpayers, already stretched thin from the industries leaving, would cover the rest. The biggest of all the contaminated sites from the former defense planets was in Bethpage at the old Grumman facility.

Most of the designated superfund sites that were relics of the Cold War defense plants or innovation hubs had no plans for cleanups until recently.

The old Republic Plant in East Farmingdale stands as a rusty tribute to the Cold War military manufacturing–based economy. These old manufacturing plants are home to the island's superfund sites. *Courtesy of Christopher Verga.*

Two cleanup plans that were recently developed with lengthy timetables were those of the Bethpage and Calverton Grumman facilities.

The Bethpage site has the largest of the underground plumes, growing at an estimated foot a week. The current underground contamination is 4.3 miles long and 2.1 miles wide 900 feet below the ground, which is believed to be the same depth of the Upper Glacial Aquifer. Long Island's three drinking water aquifers include the Upper Glacier Aquifer, Magothy Aquifer and the Lloyd Aquifer. Our source for drinking water is in the Magothy Aquifer. Magothy is 1,100 feet below the ground, and it supplies 90 percent of Nassau County's and 50 percent of Suffolk County's drinking water. The site has over twenty-four containments, including dioxane and radium. This cleanup's timetable projections are as long as one hundred years, with a growing price tag of $585 million. The state environmental officials recommended twenty-four wells pump 17.5 million gallons of water per day into five treatment plants.[166] In an effort to recoup some of the costs for a cleanup, Long Island Pure Water Ltd. filed a federal lawsuit that claims the navy leased the site to Grumman. The argument over the responsibility for the contamination is currently being fought in the courts, and due to the recent state budget crisis, the $100 million needed to start construction of the twenty-four wells is being delayed. As the residents wait patiently,

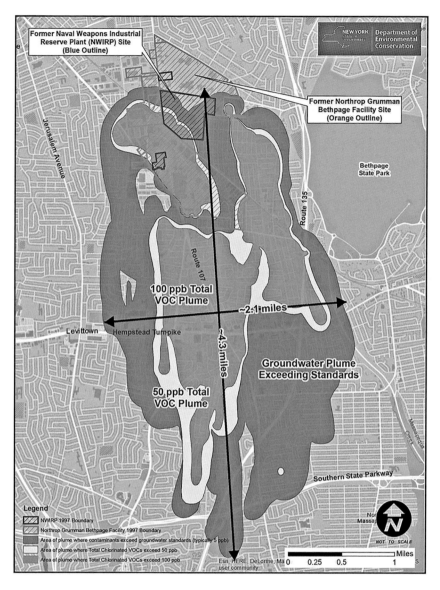

Above: Pictured is a map of the toxic plume came from decades of manufacturing at the Bethpage Plant. The plume stretched west of the Levittown Hempstead Turnpike and east of Route 135 Bethpage. *Courtesy of the New York State Department of Environmental Conservation.*

Opposite: Proposed fast-track extraction drills are set up in designated areas within the plume's radius. These drills are designed to extract the toxins from the groundwater aquifers. *Courtesy of the New York State Department of Environmental Conservation.*

the plume grows closer and closer to their main source of water, which can result in a public health disaster.

In 2009, the Grumman Calverton Plant was confirmed to have an underground plume that contained the chemical dichloroethane. The Suffolk County Health Department discovered a plume that was at least one-third of a mile wide and moving south, discharging into the Peconic River.[167] An initial assessment concluded that the plume was not a threat to groundwater. In further studies conducted at the site in 2010, a chemical known as PFAS was found in groundwater wells surrounding the plant, and the plume was larger than initially believed. The county, after discovering the contamination, also found out that Grumman had been aware of the pollution at its facility since at least 1992. In documents disclosed to district court, the findings discovered in a study done by an environmental consultant working for the navy cited a "high possibility of a threat to nearby drinking water by migration of hazardous substance in the groundwater."[168] The cleanup plan is currently unresolved, but exposure to these chemicals is linked to developmental effects on fetuses and various cancers. Currently, three thousand neighboring residents remain at immediate risk of the pollutant's effects.

The Calverton Grumman Plant is now Grumman Memorial Park. Pictured is the iconic F14, which was manufactured on the site. *Courtesy of Christopher Verga.*

The Brookhaven National Laboratory superfund site was caused by leaked radioactive tritium from two nuclear reactors, which polluted the groundwater from mid-1950s to the 1990s—until the Department of Energy (DOE) terminated its contract with Brookhaven and Associated Universities and had the reactors permanently shut down, ending their reactor program. Associated Universities group was set up in 1947 to manage BNL; it included Harvard, Yale, Princeton, Columbia, Cornell and Johns Hopkins, among other universities. Providing more radioactive contamination was the Gamma Forest Project. The Radiation Ecology Project, commonly referred to as the Gamma Forest, investigated the effects of radioactivity on organisms. A tract of 50 acres of land was exposed for twenty hours a day to a 9,500-curie-gamma source of cesium-137 (a radioactive isotope).[169] The project was expanded to 123 acres of pine and oak trees between the years of 1961 to 1979.

The severity of the waste and reckless of BNL projects surfaced through Arthur Humm. Humm began working at the laboratory in 1949, and in 1968, he was promoted to director of radiation protection at the laboratory's High Flux Beam Reactor. During the late 1970s, his brother-in-law Simon Perchik was an assistant Suffolk district attorney in charge of environmental prosecution, and on numerous occasions, he accused BNL of contaminating Suffolk County's environment. As a result, Perchik had many arguments with Humm, who defended the laboratory and its practices—until they cost him his life. One BNL practice was to pump waste out a pool, where the irradiated water from the reactor flowed, and then Humm, wearing only a face mask, would attempt to scrub away the radioactive residue from the walls of the pool with a brush. He later developed lung cancer. In 1981, a terminally ill Humm brought a multimillion-dollar lawsuit against the federal government, charging that his lung cancer was a result of inhaling radioactive particles in this process. He subsequently died—a victim, said Perchik, of the irresponsible way the national laboratory dealt with radiation.[170] "Artie, as he was dying, felt that the safeguards afforded him by the laboratory were inadequate," said Perchik. "The face mask was a very rudimentary face mask that could leak. It was the kind housepainters wear." Of BNL, Perchik said, "You have a bunch of mad scientists doing experiments in the cellar—and nobody is looking in."[171] But the worst was yet to come.

At its peak, the pollution extended underground into the hamlet of Shirley to the south of the laboratory past the Brookhaven-Calabro Airport.[172] BNL not only contaminated the land on which it sits and the underground water below, but it has also contaminated the Peconic River. Its headwaters begin at BNL, and the river feeds into a chain of bays, beginning with Flanders Bay, then Great Peconic Bay and continuing toward bays in the east. Contaminants found in the Peconic River emitted through the sewage treatment system at BNL include cesium-137, strontium-90 and tritium. According to a 1979 New York State report, radiation levels in the Peconic River were the second-highest near nuclear-related facilities in the state. Only in lakes and streams around what had been the defunct nuclear fuel reprocessing facility in West Valley were the levels higher.[173] Later, BNL claimed radioactive material in the Peconic River came from fallout from nuclear weapons testing in the western United States. "On Long Island, as anywhere else in the U.S., natural 'clean' water always contains some radiation, which comes from the fallout remaining after early atomic tests," insisted BNL director George Vineyard in 1979.[174] This contradicted BNL's claims in a 2004 report, "Peconic River Health and Environmental Assessment," which was commissioned by the Suffolk County legislature. It concluded: "Radioactive and chemical wastes [from BNL] have been 'discarded' in the facility's wastewater systems for more than forty years of laboratory operations." Commenting on the report, Bill Smith, the executive director of the organization Fish Unlimited, said the report "verifies Fish Unlimited's past statements" that the "Peconic River is a cesspool of contamination thanks to Brookhaven Lab....This is a sad confirmation of what we've known for years."[175] After decades of denial, BNL finally acknowledged in official documents and publicly that it was a major source of the radiation in the Peconic River and agreed to a cleanup. As it noted in a 2005 press release headed "Department of Energy, EPA and N.Y. State Reach Agreement on Peconic River Cleanup," the radioactive materials came through BNL's sewage treatment plant that was in operation "since the Laboratory was established in 1947."[176] The article went on to further explain that the "historical operations and disposal practices resulted in the discharge into the Peconic River of wastewater containing chemical and radiological contaminants, which were then deposited in the sediment." The first step of the cleanup included building seventy-nine extraction wells that would remove the plume by 2070. The $365 million cost of the cleanup was covered by the federal government. For the Peconic, a removal of six to twelve inches of contaminated river sediment and deposits will remove and estimated 92 percent of the mercury and PCBs in the river. The cost to the labs will be $11.5 million. However, despite the agreement to cover the costs, the surrounding communities became plagued with higher-than-normal cancer rates. The communities of Shirley, Mastic and Mastic Beach suffered the brunt of the pollution. Research by Dr. Jay M. Gould, a cofounder of the Radiation Public Health Project and a former member of the EPA Science Advisory Board, discovered, based on National Cancer Institute data, that those areas around seven U.S. national nuclear laboratories had an increase in age-adjusted breast cancer mortality between 1950 and 1989. This is an average jump of 35 percent, compared to a one percent national rise. In Suffolk County, there was a 40 percent hike in breast cancer rates. Suffolk had "the biggest increase in age-adjusted breast cancer mortality during this period for any single large county in the U.S.," said Gould, and he attributed this to BNL. The communities closest to BNL had the largest incidence of cancer.[177] Worsening the reality of the breast cancer data was the children's cancer cluster that emerged in year 2000, with children afflicted by a series of rare soft-tissue cancers.[178] From the data and the growing amount of cancer victims, a $1 billion lawsuit was filed against BNL for the effects of the radioactive contamination. During the publications of the studies related to the cancer clusters, the state DEC found that deer on the ground or in the surrounding communities of the labs had high levels of radioactivity.

Following a new finding, a radioactive materials technician, Kenneth Dobreuenaski, who worked in the lab, emerged as a whistleblower in 1996. In an interview, he stated, "If people knew about what really goes on at Brookhaven National Laboratory, they'd make the lab clean it up—and do it damn fast." He said, "There's no accountability at the lab. You have to understand the mentality of some of the scientists there. They'd roll around in a pile of plutonium."[179] After becoming a whistleblower, Dobreuenaski was pressured to resign in an effort to silence him.

Lead attorneys for the plaintiffs, Richard J. Lippes, whose Buffalo, New York law firm successfully represented the residents of the Love Canal neighborhood near Niagara Falls, which was severely polluted by the Hooker Chemical Company, and A. Craig Purcell, a former president of the Suffolk County Bar Association, took up a case relating to the lab's negligence. This lawsuit's title is *Osarczuk v. Associated Universities*. Barbra Osarczuk had lived in North Shirley, just outside the BNL boundaries, for twenty-eight years and attributed her thyroid and breast cancer to BNL. She told journalist Karl Grossman that her neighborhood was a hotbed of cancer and that BNL had "tried to cover this up." Randy Snell of Manorville, another plaintiff, said his daughter developed rhabdomyosarcoma, a cancer that developed in her mouth and throat, that was attributed to BNL. Snell, in a 1996 interview with Karl Grossman, stated, "The more we look into Brookhaven pollution, the more we discover." In a follow-up interview with the attorney, Purcell said that BNL "successfully delayed" court action on the lawsuit through the decades. "They appealed everything."[180] In settlement negotiations, the plaintiffs were divided into three groups, each with about eighteen persons. BNL has agreed to settlements of approximately $600,000 for two groups. The third group, as of 2020, some twenty-four years after the suit was filed, was still awaiting a resolution. The compensation has been far from the $1 billion originally sought. However, at one point, in an appeal by BNL lawyers to the Appellate Division of the New York State Supreme Court, the BNL lawyers, argued "The nuclear radiation emitted by BNL did not exceed guidelines promulgated by the federal Nuclear Regulatory Commission." The court agreed.

Radioactive contamination caused by BNL was further documented in the 2008 book *Welcome to Shirley: A Memoir from an Atomic Town*, authored by Professor Kelly McMasters of Hofstra University. The book was the basis of the 2012 TV documentary *Atomic States of America*. As McMasters, raised in Shirley, related in a 2012 interview:

I do believe there was a watershed moment in 1960, after the first radioactive leaks occurred, that the federal government or the scientists themselves should have realized that Shirley was the fastest growing town in the county, with a population that doubled within ten years, and that the middle of one of the largest sole-source drinking water aquifers in the country was not the best place for a nuclear laboratory.

Meanwhile, the U.S. government began paying out millions of dollars to BNL employees in compensation for getting cancer from their exposure to radioactivity at BNL, and it began providing compensation to families of BNL workers who had died from BNL-linked cancer. The payouts to the BNL workers and families has come under the federal Energy Employees Occupational Illness Compensation Program, which covers not only BNL but the string of U.S. national nuclear laboratories, including Los Alamos, Livermore and Oak Ridge Labs and the federal Savannah River Plant and Hanford Site. According to the BNL Employee Occupational Illness Compensation Program, in 2012, some $8.2 billion was set aside for payouts, with $111.7 million for exposures to radioactivity and consequent cancer at BNL.

Throughout the decades, BNL scientists have minimized the dangers of nuclear technology and radiation. A BNL flier distributed in the 1990s, for example, declared: "We live in a radioactive world—radiation is all around us and is part of our natural environment." Or, as a laboratory booklet long distributed to BNL personnel, *The ABCs of Radiation*, states: "Is Radiation Dangerous to You? It can be; but it need not be." The booklet compares radiation to fire and electricity. "We have learned to live with these agents," it says, "and we can learn to live with radiation."[181]

By the mid-1990s, the Cold War boom of Long Island was a fading memory. The old rusted structures of Republic Aviation and the Bethpage Grumman Plant, Great River Grumman Plant and Calverton Plant stood as a testament to a once-booming economy. The tax base that these plants once paid shifted to residential homes, due to much of the land being redeveloped into residential housing. This void in a commercial tax base ballooned Long Island property taxes to become some of the highest in the nation. In addition to shifting the tax base to homeowners, unenforced environmental laws for Cold War industries left the horrific relic of polluted estuaries and hazards to our aquifers. Economic progress of a few decades came at the cost of high cancer rates for many Long Islanders. The island's natural beauty that had remained intact for thousands of years became a dotted landscape of capes

This page: The old Cold War–era military base Camp Hero was closed in the mid-1980s and became a state park in 2002. The old gun emplacements remain relics of Cold War militarization. *Courtesy of Christopher Verga.*

with manicured lawns. Other picturesque landscapes were transformed into either blighted factory skeletons or superfund sites due to decades of pollution. While wreaking havoc on the natural resources, the gross domestic state product (GDP) for Long Island was estimated, at one point, to be larger than twenty-one of the fifty states' GDP. It would take Long Island until 2007 to reach this economic milestone again.[182] The overall effect of the Cold War's end was the island's true test in remarketing its identity and building back a stronger economy that would not put the health of its residents at risk. Following the departure of Cold War industries, the number of Nassau and Suffolk residents who worked in the city went from 423,000 in 1960 to 992,000 in 2000.[183] The increasing dependency on the city workers may make the island seem more like a dorm to the city, but these numbers do not reflect Long Island's recent economic diversification. The Hauppauge Industrial Park, in the last forty years, has expanded to be one of the largest in the country, with over one thousand companies occupying the space. In addition, CA Technologies, at one time, made its home in Long Island and introduced the region to the multibillion-dollar tech industry.

Built from the postwar idealism and contradictions, the region endured. Nevertheless, the resilience of Long Island was tested, and it has risen to national economic and social prominence not once but twice. It became a region that refused to except defeat—to become another rust belt dotted with superfund sites.

NOTES

1. Lake Success Failures at the United Nations

1. Ben White, "Mayor Urges Lake Success Welcome UN: Vote on Saturday," *Newsday*, April 18, 1946, 3.
2. United States Office of the Historian, "The Acheson-Lilienthal & Baruch Plans, 1946," October 15, 2011, www.history.state.gov.
3. Staff writer, "UN Reopens A-Bomb Control," *Newsday*, September 27, 1946, 56.
4. Staff writer, "Manchausen at Lake Success," *Newsday*, November 15, 1949, 31.
5. Staff writer, "World-Wide: Deadline in Lake Success," *Newsday*, November 7, 1950, 2.
6. James Edwin, "Reds Get Bit Tangled on Korean Volunteers; Vishinsky at Lake Success Sticks to His Yarn While Peiping Radio Calls for Bigger Aid," *New York Times*, December 10, 1950, E3.
7. Staff writer, "At the UN, a Wordless Debate," *Newsday*, December 8, 1950, 2.
8. Ibid.
9. Staff writer, "UN, Striving for Peace, Begins Vacating Plant Needed for War," *Newsday*, August 19, 1950, 2.

2. Birth of Levittown, America: Living on the Edge

10. Joshua Pearce and David Denkenberger, "A National Pragmatic Safety Limit for Nuclear Weapon Quantities," *Safety* 4, no. 2 (2018): 25.

11. Staff writer, "Albany Gets Bill for Bomb Shelters, Local Aid," *Newsday*, March 3, 1951, 48.

12. Otto Ninow, "Bomb Shelters or Pools: What's the Choice," *Newsday*, July 17, 1959, 29.

13. Henry Brooks, "But How Do We Pay for the Bomb Shelters," *Newsday*, August 31, 1959, 25.

14. Staff writer, "Bombs and Shelters," *Newsday*, October 18, 1961, 49.

15. Rebecca Onion, "The Teacher Would Suddenly Yell Drop," *Slate*, March 13, 2018, 3.

16. Ibid.

17. Edwin Ritche, "Are Bomb Shelters an Encouragement for War?" *Newsday*, December 15, 1960, 53.

18. Herbert Ruben, "Readers Ask Disarmament, Not Bomb Shelters," *Newsday*, February 26, 1960, 39.

19. Steven Mintz and Susan Kellogg, "Domestic Revolutions: A Social History of American Family Life," *Free Press*, 1989, 207.

20. Staff writer, "Unsettling Facts About Tranquilizers," Consumer Reports, January 1958, 4.

21. Stephanie Coontz, *The Way We Never Were: American Families and the Nostalgia Trap* (New York: Basic Books, 1992), 32.

22. Herbert Gans, *The Levittowners: Ways of Life and Politics in a New Suburban Community* (New York: Columbia University Press, 1967), 37.

23. John Moscow, "I Guess Most of the Groups in School Regard Me as the Village Idiot," *Newsday*, May 1, 1965, 12W.

24. Carole Ashinaze, "LI Civil Rights Group Spurred on by Critics," *Newsday*, December 4, 1968, 3A.

25. Michael Stern, "Anti-Negro Group Loosely Formed: SPONGE Members Are Whites in Interracial Areas," *New York Times*, July 23, 1966, 8.

3. Military Industrial Complex of Long Island

26. Staff writer, "Republic Slashes Time, Cost of Thunderbolts," *Newsday*, January 11, 1945, 3.

27. Helen Dudar, "Fear Republic Mass Layoffs Prelude to Air Industry Slump," *Newsday*, May 24, 1947, 2.

28. Delaware Corporation, Annual Report 1955 Republic Aviation Corporation, Farmingdale, New York, March 23, 1956, 12.

29. Ibid., 14

30. Richard Aurelio, "Ousters Threaten New Republic Strike," *Newsday*, June 5, 1952, 43.

31. Staff writer, "Republic Strike Deadline Nears," *Newsday*, February 18, 1954, 1.

32. Bill Butler, "Agreement Averts Strike at Republic," *Newsday*, February 21, 1955, 5.

33. Staff writer, "Senate Unit Says It's Looking Into Republic Strike," *Newsday*, May 17, 1956, 7.

34. Frank Johnson, "Perfall Art, Republic Strike Near End, 2 Technicalities Last Snag," *Newsday*, June 2, 1956, 3.

35. Staff writer, "Cuts at Republic Force Subcontractor Layoffs," *Newsday*, October 10, 1957, 7.

36. Arnold Brophy, "Island Takes Lead in Missile Age," *Newsday*, January 25, 1958, 36M.

37. Stan Brooks, "Fairchild Sells Plant to Republic Corp. in Multi-Million $ Deal," *Newsday*, July 30, 1954, 3.

38. Art Bergmann and Maurice Swift, "Suffolk to Buy Republic Airfield," *Newsday*, June 14, 1966, 2.

39. Staff writer, "Court Upsets 60-G Tax Bill Against Grumman Plant," *Newsday*, December 15, 1956, 17.

40. Tom Renner and Art Perfall, "Navy Asks Ban on Housing Near Grumman Jet Field," *Newsday*, August 4, 1956, 3.

41. Ralph Weyant, Christopher Verga interview with former mechanic with Grumman, Bay Shore, NY, October 21, 2020.

42. Pranay Gupte, "Has Grumman Pulled Out of Its Tailspin?" *Newsday*, January 19, 1975, 145.

4. Long Island's Race to the Moon

43. CIA, "The Kitchen Debate—Transcript, July 24, 1959, Vice President Richard Nixon and Soviet Nikita Khrushchev, U.S. Embassy, Moscow, Soviet Union," www.cia.gov.

44. Val Duncan, "Assignment: The Moon," *Newsday*, September 4, 1962, 1C.

45. Michael Dorman, "Grumman Will Build Moon Bug, LI Seen as Future Space Center," *Newsday*, November 8, 1962, 3.

46. George Wheeler, "Ted K. Reaches for Grumman's Moon," *Newsday*, December 10, 1962, 7.

47. Thomas Kelly, "NASA Johnson Space Center Oral History Project Edited Oral History Transcript," interview by Kevin Rusnak, Cutchogue, New York, September 19, 2000.

48. Thomas Collins, "Grumman Gets Billion for Moon Craft," *Newsday*, February 15, 1966, 1.

49. John Wilford, "Wernher von Braun, Rocket Pioneer, Dies," *New York Times*, June 18, 1977, 1, www.nytimes.com.

50. Kelly, interview.

51. Staff writer, "Snag Delays Moon Module Test: 11th Hour Snag Holds Test of Moon Module," *Newsday*, January 22, 1968, 2.

52. Henry Cooper, "Moon Car, the Talk of the Town," *New York Times*, January 18, 1969, 25.

53. Grumman Aerospace Corporation, Forty-Second Annual Report, 1971, 12.

5. Secret Weapons and Human Experiments

54. Atomic Heritage Foundation, "Letter from Enrico Fermi to Einstein, August 1939, Nassau Point, Long Island, New York," July 18, 2017, www.atomicheritage.org.

55. Custer Institute, "Letter from Einstein to Roosevelt Describing the Work of Enrico Fermi and L. Szilard, August 2, 1939, Nassau Point, Long Island, New York," www.custerobservatory.org.

56. James Kunetka, *City of Fire* (Albuquerque: University of New Mexico Press, 1978), 38.

57. Glenn Alcalay, "Human Radiation Experiments in the Pacific," *CounterPunch*, March 3, 2014, www.jfortin670.wixsite.com.

58. Letter from Nina Latobe for the testimony in 1984 before a subcommittee of the Committee on Appropriations of the U.S. House of Representatives, Ninety-Eighth Congress, second session, subcommittee of the Department of the Interior and related agencies, Washington, D.C., 1984.

59. Letter from Arta Rijon for the testimony in 1984 before a subcommittee of the Committee on Appropriations of the U.S. House of

Representatives, Ninety-Eighth Congress, second session, subcommittee on the Department of the Interior and Related Agencies, Washington, D.C., 1984.

60. Staff writer, "Phyllis Vineyard, A Consultant, 72," *New York Times*, March 24, 1996, section 1, 48.

61. Ann Mead, interviewed by Karl Grossman, December 1985; New York State Public Service Commission, 1948 Annual Report and press release, Consolidated Edison Company, December 10, 1948.

62. Karl Grossman, *Power Crazy: Is LILCO Turing Shoreham Into America's Chernobyl?* (New York: Grove Press, 1986), 188.

63. Karl Grossman, "The Rise and Fall of LILCO's Nuclear Program," *Long Island History Journal* 5, no. 1 (Fall 1992): 10.

64. Irving Like, interviewed by Karl Grossman, Bay Shore, NY, November 1967.

65. Diamond Stuart, "Hearings Put Nuclear Power on Trial," *Newsday*, November 15, 1981, 29.

66. A Facsimile Report, United States Energy Research and Development Administration, Technical Information Center, Oak Ridge, TN, www.dissident-media.org.

67. Lester L. Wolff, interviewed by Karl Grossman, Brookhaven, NY, December 1985.

68. Michio Kaku, interviewed by Karl Grossman, Brookhaven, NY, May 1979.

69. Steve Wick, "N-Plant Memos Routine," *Newsday*, December 4, 1979, 4.

70. Testimony of George W. Henry and Ronald Stanchfield before the Suffolk County Legislature, January 30, 1985.

71. Mathew Wald, "Amid Debates, Shoreham Plant Sits in Silence," *New York Times*, September 29, 1984, 25.

72. John Herrington, "The Challenger for Nuclear Power," Nuclear Power Assembly, May 6, 1985, Washington, D.C.

73. Karl Grossman, interviewed by Tom Twomey, Brookhaven, NY, January 1992.

74. Editorial board, "As Shoreham Goes," *Nation*, June 11, 1988.

75. Staff writer, "Long Island's Oystermen Are Not in favor of Plum Island Lab," *Newsday*, August 14, 1952, 7.

76. Michael Carroll, *Lab 257: The Story of the Government's Secret Plum Island Germ Laboratory* (New York: HarperCollins, 2004), 45.

77. John McDonald, "Plum Island's Shadowy Past," *Newsday*, November 21, 1993, 2.

78. Ibid., A5.

79. Ibid.

80. Carroll, *Lab 257*, 32.

81. Ibid.

82. Drew Featherston and John Cummings, "Cuban Outbreak of Swine Fever Linked to CIA," *Newsday*, January 9, 1977, 2.

83. Boyce Rensberger, "U.S. Plum Island Lab Holds Its First Open House," *New York Times*, October 24, 1971, 53.

84. John Loftus, *The Belarus Secret: The Nazi Connection in America* (New York: Knopf, 1982).

85. U.S. Government Accountability Office, "Combating Bio-Terrorism: Action Needed to Improve Security at Plum Island Animal Disease Center," September 19, 2003, www.gao.gov.

86. Karl Grossman, "Target: Plum Island," *New York Times*, September 11, 2005, www.nytimes.com.

87. Michael Carroll, interviewed by Karl Grossman, Sag Harbor, NY, October 2013.

6. Russian Spies in the Shadows of Suburbia

88. Annie Jacobsen, *Operation Paperclip: The Secret Intelligence Program to Bring Nazi Scientists to America* (New York: Little, Brown and Company, 2014), 500.

89. CIA, "The Office of Scientific Intelligence 1949–68, Volume 2, Annexes IV, V, VI, June 1972, 3," www.cia.gov.

90. CIA, "Memorandum for Project 63 Personal Now in the U.S. Reference Col. B. Heckemyer, Chief JIOA on December 29, 1951," www.cia.gov.

91. *Newsday* Washington Bureau, "Washington Asks JFK to Help Glen Cove in Tax Dispute with Russians," *Newsday*, December 14, 1961, 28.

92. Sam Roberts, *The Brother: The Untold Story of the Rosenberg Case* (New York: Random House, 2003), 509.

93. Ibid., 425–26.

94. CIA, "Letter from Mayor Alan Parente to William Casey, April 28, 1982," www.cia.gov.

95. Bob Caro, "Huge LI Security Force Waits K," *Newsday*, September 24, 1960, 3.

96. George Wheeler, "Nikita Coming to Long Island for the Week-End," *Newsday*, September 23, 1960, 2.

97. Jim Neil and Don O'Drake, "K. Draw LI Crowds: They Can't See Him: 5,000 on Long Island Don't See Khrusk," *Newsday*, September 26, 1960, 5.

98. Ibid.

99. Staff writer, "Khrushchev Says Soviet Is Ready to Put an Astronaut into Space: Soviet Is Ready for Man in Space," *New York Times*, September 26, 1960, 1.

100. Kathleen Teltsch, "Algerians to See Soviet Premier," *New York Times*, October 2, 1960, 13.

101. Staff writer, "K. Urges Algeria To Fight France," *Newsday*, October 3, 1960, 2.

102. Ernie Volkmann and Phil Ross, "Just a Neighbor—With a Difference," *Newsday*, January 8, 1965, 38.

103. Staff writer, "FBI Nabs LI Man as Spy for Reds," *Newsday*, January 7, 1965, 1.

104. Harvey Aronson and Philip Ross, "How One Man Sold Out His Country," *Newsday*, March 1965, 20.

105. David Anderson, "3 Russians are Accused as Co-Conspirators in Ring," *New York Times*, January 8, 1965, 1.

106. Aronson and Ross, "One Man," 21.

107. Ronald Maiorana, "Thompson Denies Spy Charges and Says He's 100% American," *New York Times*, January 9, 1965, 3.

108. Ronald Maiorana, "L.I. Spy Tells of Serving Soviet," *New York Times*, March 9, 1965, 1.

109. Ibid., 25.

110. Aronson and Ross, "One Man," 22.

111. Ronald Maiorana, "Ex-Airman Given 30 Years: As a Spy," *Newsday*, May 14, 1965, 7.

112. Samuel Bruchey, "A Patriot's Cold War Tale/Long Island Man Recalls Role as U.S. Counterspy," *Newsday*, February 18, 2002, A3.

113. Staff writer, "Spying Charges Quashed Against Soviet Translator," *New York Times*, August 16, 1972, 40.

114. Joseph Treen, "LI Throngs Protest Red Trials," *Newsday*, January 4, 1971, 1.

115. Lynn Rosellini, "Jews Claim Raid on Red Estate," *Newsday*, July 28, 1970, 3.

116. Robert Reno, "U.S. Warns DiPaola on Move to Collect Taxes from Soviets: DiPaola Warned on Tax Move," *Newsday*, July 24, 1970, 3.

117. Joseph Treen, "3 Indicted in Bomb at Killenworth," *Newsday* September 1971, 17.

118. Sylvia Moreno, "Firstman Richard, Soviets Said to spy on LI Firms," *Newsday*, April 28, 1982, 7.

119. Sylvia Moreno, "Curb by Glen Cove on Soviets Irks US," *Newsday*, July 21, 1982, 16.
120. Staff writer, "Glen Cove Holds to Soviet Ban," *Newsday*, August 7, 1982, 3.
121. Jamie Schram and Jennifer Bain, "Russian Compound Shut Down Over Election Hack," *New York Post*, December 30, 2016, www.nypost.com.
122. Lauren Gambino, "US-Russian Tensions Rise as Malware Found at Vermont Electric Utility," *Guardian*, December 31, 2016, www.theguardian.com.

7. Buildup of Military and Nuclear Missile Bases on Long Island

123. Hal Levy, "Air Force Turns Down Pleas to Move Mitchell Field," *Newsday*, November 4, 1955, 3.
124. Arnold Bropby and Harvey Aronson, "Air Force May Close Mitchel Field," *Newsday*, April 9, 1958, 1.
125. Christopher Bright, *Continental Defense in the Eisenhower Era, Nuclear Antiaircraft Arms and the Cold War* (New York: Palgrave Macmillan, 2010), 9.
126. Tom Morris, "Nike—U.S. Cities Last Line of Defense," *Newsday*, March 11, 1957, 10C.
127. Joseph Berger, "Shadow Cast by Region's Atomic Past," *New York Times*, July 31, 2009.
128. Vivian Toy, "The Island's Nuclear-Tipped Past: From Amityville to Rocky Point, Missile Sites Held Cold War Secrets," *New York Times*, May 28, 2000, www.nytimes.com.
129. Ibid.
130. Bernie Bookbinder, "Army Halts Plans for LI Nike Work," *Newsday*, May 23, 1958, 3.
131. Berger, "Shadow."
132. Bill Bleyer, "The Russians Were Coming, and Long Island Was Ready with a String of Cold War Defense, Some of Which Can Still Be Seen Today," *Newsday*, March 10, 2002, G06.

8. America's Cold War Conflicts Become Wars

133. Staff writer, "Dead GI's Kin See Mme. Nhu," *Newsday*, October 16, 1963, 4.

134. George Motz, interviewed by Christopher Verga, Bay Shore, NY, September 15, 2020.

135. George Motz, *Taps, The Silent Victims of the Vietnam War: The Families Left Behind* (Southampton, NY: Peconic Bay Publishing, 2019), 23–24.

136. Frank Romero, interviewed by Christopher Verga, Bay Shore, NY, September 1, 2020.

137. Staff writer, "A Chronology of Death: 1965," *Newsday*, August 2, 1969, 10W.

138. James Truax, interviewed by Christopher Verga, Bay Shore, NY, September 10, 2020.

139. Carole Ashkinaze and Lewis Grossberger, "Moratorium Today for War Foes: Capitalizing on Protest Foes," *Newsday*, October 15, 1969, 2.

140. Lewis Grossberger, "Peace Tide Sweeps Across Long Island as Thousands Protest Vietnam," *Newsday*, October 16, 1969, 28.

141. Bill Hughes, interviewed by Christopher Verga, Bay Shore, NY, November 12, 2020.

142. Staff writer, "Hofstra Students Sit in to Seek Power, Peace," *Newsday*, April 15, 1970, 8.

143. Les Payne, Paul Schreiber and Earl Lane, "State University Protest Hits Draft Office," *Newsday*, May 7, 1970, 5.

144. David Andelman, "Town Turns out to Greet A P.O.W.," *New York Times*, March 20, 1973, 8, www.nytimes.com.

145. Jack Parente, interviewed by Christopher Verga, Bay Shore, NY, November 1, 2020.

146. Hughes, interview.

9. Eroded Trust and the Rise of Long Island's Rust Belt

147. Oriana Fallaci, "Otis Pike and the CIA Interview," *New Republic*, April 3, 1976, 11.

148. White House memo between Donald Rumsfeld and Jim Connor, subject: the intelligence community, September 12, 1975, National Security Archive at George Washington University.

149. Letter to Otis Pike from CIA director W.E. Colby, October 14, 1975, National Security Archive at George Washington University.

150. Aaron Lantham, "The CIA Report the President Doesn't Want You to Read, Pike Papers: Highlights from the Suppressed House Intelligence Committee Report," *Village Voice*, February 16, 1976, A24, www.villagevoice.com.

151. Art Buchwald, "How Spies Secrets Become Stock Tips for the CIA's Casey," *Newsday*, June 9, 1983, 91.

152. Patrick Tyler, "Casey Cleared by U.S. in Foreign Agent Case," *Newsday*, April 9, 1982, 5.

153. C-SPAN, "Interview on C-SPAN, Victor Yannacone, Agent Orange and Coming Home to War," April 19, 2001, www.c-span.org.

154. Ibid.

155. Victor Yannacone, interviewed by Christopher Verga, Bay Shore, NY, September 21, 2020.

156. Adrian Peracchio, "Dow Tries to Merge Vets' Suits," *Newsday*, March 21, 1979, 7.

157. Staff writer, "Judgement on Herbicides Viewed as Job of Environment Agency," *New York Times*, August 16, 1979, D18.

158. James Sparrow, interviewed by Christopher Verga, Bay Shore, NY, September 16, 2020.

159. Ralph Blumenthal, "Veterans Accept $180 Million on Agent Orange," *New York Times*, May 8, 1984, section A,

160. Staff writer, "Cracks in the Grumman Image: Problems Plaque the Company's Flexible Buses is Cited as Replacement Head for New York," *Newsday*, December 21, 1980, 4.

161. James Bernstein, "Clipped Wings: Fairchild's T-46A Jet Loses Funds After Debate, D'Amato Filibuster," *Newsday*, October 18, 1986, 1.

162. Daniel Cuff, "Dark Days for Fairchild Unit," *New York Times*, September 5, 1985, section D, 1.

163. James Bernstein, "Grumman Decides Against Buying Fairchild-Republic," *Newsday*, December 13, 1985, 1.

164. James Bernstein, "Fairchild Plant Closing," *Newsday*, March 14, 1987, 5.

165. James Bernstein, "LI Delivers Its Last 7-14 Tomcat's Departure Closes an Era for Island and Grumman, Leaving Behind an Uncertain Economic Future," *Newsday*, July 2, 1992, 21.

166. David Schwartz, "A Plan to Stanch Bethpage Plume," *Newsday*, May 24, 2019, 2.

167. Jennifer Smith, "A Push for Cleanup Schumer Joining in Call for Action by Navy on Polluted Plume from Ex-Grumman Site in Calverton that Threatens the Peconic River," *Newsday*, March 30, 2009, A6.

168. Paul LaRocco and David Schwartz, "2 Plumes: 1 Growing, 1 Receding," *Newsday*, July 26, 2020, 2.

169. BNL Personnel Office, "The BNL Gamma Forest," *Bulletin Board* 15, no. 19 (January 16, 1962): 1–2.

170. Grossman, *Power Crazy*, 183–84.

171. Simon Perchik, interviewed by Karl Grossman, Brookhaven, NY, February 1986.

172. LaRocco and Schwartz, "2 Plumes," 2.

173. Staff writer, "Brookhaven's Radioactivity," *East Hampton Star*, March 29, 1979.

174. Karl Grossman, "BNL Director Answers," *Long Island Advance*, March 30, 1979, 34, www.nyshistoricnewspapers.org.

175. Bill Smith, interviewed by Karl Grossman, Brookhaven, NY, March 31, 2004.

176. Brookhaven National Laboratory, "Department of Energy, Environmental Protection Agency and New York State Reach Agreement on Peconic River Cleanup," February 15, 2005, www.bnl.gov.

177. Jay Gould, *The Enemy Within: The High Cost of Living Near Nuclear Reactors* (New York: Four Walls Eight Windows, 1996), 82.

178. Kelly McMasters, "The Nuclear Neighborhood," *New York Times*, November 12, 2006, www.nytimes.com.

179. Kenneth Dobreunaski, interviewed by Karl Grossman, Brookhaven, NY, February 12, 1996.

180. A. Craig Purcell, interviewed by Karl Grossman, Brookhaven, NY, August 22, 2020.

181. Karl Grossman, *The ABCs of Radiation: Brookhaven National Laboratory as a Facsimile in Cover Up* (New York: Permanent Press, 1980), 85–91.

182. Staff writer, "How Long Island Would Rank as 51st State," *Newsday*, May 16, 2009, www.newsday.com.

183. Phillip Lutz, "Lobbying to Keep Economic Identity," *New York Times*, July 20, 2003, www.nytimes.com.

ABOUT THE AUTHORS

Christopher Verga is an instructor of Long Island history and foundations of American history at Suffolk Community College and a contributor to the online local news sites Greater Babylon, Greater Bay Shore and Greater Patchogue. His published works include *Images of American Series Civil Rights Movement on Long Island*, *Images of American Series Bay Shore* and *Saving Fire Island from Robert Moses*. Christopher has his educational doctorate degree from St John's University. His dissertation work included research on Long Island Native Americans and the impact of tribal recognition within their cultural identity.

Karl Grossman is a full professor of journalism at the State University of New York/College at Old Westbury. He has specialized in investigative reporting in a variety of media for more than fifty years. He is based on Long Island and formerly did investigative reporting and wrote a column for the daily *Long Island Press*. His column has appeared in weekly Long Island newspapers and on Long Island news websites since the *Long Island Press* ceased publication. Books he has authored include *Cover Up: What You Are Not Supposed to Know About Nuclear Power*; *The Wrong Stuff: The Space Program's Nuclear Threat to Our Planet*; *Weapons in Space*; and *Power Crazy: Is LILCO Turning Shoreham Into America's Chernobyl?* He founded and was the first president of the Press Club of Long Island. He was selected to be in the original class of its Long Island Journalism Hall of Fame. He has also been cited by it as "Long Island Journalist of the Year." Other honors Grossman has received for his journalism include Long Island University's George Polk Memorial Award and the Generoso Pope, James Aronson, Leo Goodman and John Peter Zenger Awards. He was a host of *Long Island World* on WLIW-TV, Long Island's PBS station, and was a co-anchor of the evening news on WSNL-TV, Long Island's commercial TV station. He was chief investigative reporter for Long Island–based WVVH-TV. He is the host of *Environment Long Island* on LTV, airing from Wainscott, Long Island. Since 1991, he has been the host of the nationally aired TV program *Enviro Close-Up with Karl Grossman*. He has written and presented many TV documentaries, including *Three Mile Island Revisited*, *The Push to Revive Nuclear Power and Nukes in Space: The Nuclearization* and *Weaponization of the Heavens*.

Visit us at
www.historypress.com